Stories of Gilbert and Sullivan Operas

Stories of Gilbert and Sullivan Operas

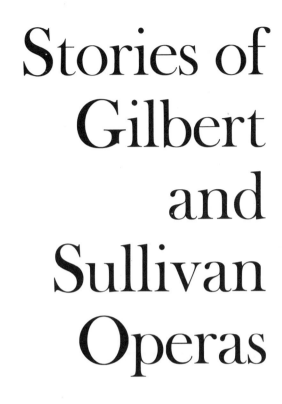

By Clyde Robert Bulla

Illustrated by James & Ruth McCrea

THOMAS Y. CROWELL COMPANY · *New York*

To Leah and Arthur

Designed by James & Ruth McCrea

Manufactured in the United States of America

L.C. Card 68-24583

1 2 3 4 5 6 7 8 9 10

Books About Opera by the Author

~§

THE RING AND THE FIRE
  Stories from Wagner's Nibelung Operas

STORIES OF FAVORITE OPERAS

MORE STORIES OF FAVORITE OPERAS

STORIES OF GILBERT AND SULLIVAN OPERAS

Copy 1

Contents

Gilbert and Sullivan   1

Trial by Jury   13
Lyrics 177

The Sorcerer   21
Lyrics 180

H.M.S. Pinafore   33
Lyrics 185

The Pirates of Penzance   49
Lyrics 194

Patience   65
Lyrics 200

Iolanthe   81
Lyrics 206

Princess Ida   97
Lyrics 211

The Mikado   111
Lyrics 216

Ruddigore   129
Lyrics 223

The Yeomen of the Guard   145
Lyrics 230

The Gondoliers   163
Lyrics 235

Index   241
Index of First Lines   245

Gilbert and Sullivan

~§ One day in the fall of 1870 a composer and an author were rehearsing a musical play they had written for the London stage. The composer was Fred Clay. The author was William S. Gilbert. A friend of Clay's, Arthur Sullivan, dropped by to watch the rehearsal, and Clay introduced him to the author.

It was the first meeting of Gilbert and Sullivan, although both men moved in London theatrical circles and each knew the work of the other. Gilbert was well known as a writer of stage pieces and humorous verse. Sullivan was one of England's most promising young composers.

The meeting was casual, yet it was momentous. It began an association that linked the names of Gilbert and Sullivan, carried them together to fame, and changed the course of English musical theater.

Gilbert was the older of the two. He was born in London on November 18, 1836. His father was a naval surgeon and a man of some means. When Gilbert was a baby, the family traveled to Italy. There, in Naples, a pair of brigands kidnapped him and held him for a ransom of twenty-five pounds. This romantic adventure impressed him deeply (afterward he claimed to remember the actual kidnapping), and stolen babies figured in more than one of the operas he was to write.

He went to school in France and England. He enjoyed writing plays and seeing his fellow students perform them, but for the most part he had little liking for school life.

He took his degree at King's College, Cambridge, then went to work as a clerk in a government office. This was no more to his liking than school. After four years an aunt left him an inheritance of four hundred pounds, and he was able to escape forever from the drudgery of his clerkship.

He studied law and was admitted to the bar, but clients did not beat a path to his door. While waiting for legal business to come his way, he wrote articles and made drawings for magazines. He began to write and illustrate for a new periodical called *Fun*. Many of his *Fun* verses he signed "Bab," his nickname when he was a child. Some of these were later collected and became famous as the *Bab Ballads*.

After four years of practicing law, he closed his office to concentrate on writing. Since his school days he had been drawn to the theater. Gradually he gave up writing for magazines and wrote plays instead.

In 1866 his first play was produced. The following year he married the daughter of an officer in the British Indian army.

Gilbert wrote play after play, both successes and failures. By the time he and Sullivan met, he had made a name for himself as a dramatist.

Arthur Sullivan was born in London on May 13, 1842. His father was a musician and managed to make a bare living by teaching, copying music, and playing in orchestras. Young Arthur grew up in an atmosphere of music. He went to rehearsals with his father and soon learned to play most of the instruments in the orchestra.

He was sent to school at a private academy. When he was twelve he won a place for himself in the Royal Choristers, a group of boys who sang at religious services in St. James's Palace. As members of the choir, they were fed and clothed, lodged, and given an education. What appealed most to Arthur was the musical education, which was an important part of his training.

When he was fourteen he won the Mendelssohn Scholarship, which gave him a year's study at the Royal Academy of Music. The following year he won again. The third year the scholarship committee voted to send him to Germany to study at the Leipzig Conservatory.

Sullivan was there for the next two and a half years. He had gone with the idea of becoming a pianist, but after a short time he turned to composition.

Back in England, he made friends who helped introduce his music to the public. He composed songs, orchestral pieces,

a solemn oratorio, and a giddy operetta. Quickly he established himself as a successful composer. He was a social success as well, and mingled with royalty on the friendliest
terms.

This was Sullivan's situation when he was introduced to
Gilbert in 1870.

W.S. Gilbert.

The next year they were at work on their first collaboration, a light opera called *Thespis, or The Gods Grown Old.* Its first performance was in London on December 23, 1871. Within a month it disappeared from the stage. Even the manuscript disappeared, and no complete copy has ever been found.

With *Thespis* a failure, Gilbert and Sullivan went their separate ways. Three years later they met again. The man who brought them together was Richard D'Oyly Carte.

D'Oyly Carte was head of a dramatic agency. He managed the careers of famous musicians, actors, and playwrights. He was also manager of the Royalty Theatre in London.

Early in 1875 he needed a short piece to produce on the same bill with the French operetta *La Périchole*. He had been impressed by *Thespis*, in spite of its failure, and he asked Gilbert if he and Sullivan could write something for the new production.

Gilbert had already written the words of a one-act opera, *Trial by Jury*. He took this libretto to Sullivan, who set it to music. The little opera was performed with such success that it outshone *La Périchole*.

D'Oyly Carte had high hopes for the future of the new team. He signed Gilbert and Sullivan to a contract giving himself managership of the company that would produce all their forthcoming operas.

But at that time Gilbert was more interested in writing plays, and Sullivan was in great demand as a conductor. Also Sullivan was suffering from ill health and from a personal tragedy. His older brother, Frederic, who sang a leading role in *Trial by Jury*, had died.

So it was more than two years after their first success before Gilbert and Sullivan finished another opera. This was *The Sorcerer*. D'Oyly Carte had taken his company from the Royalty Theatre to the Opéra Comique Theatre, and *The Sorcerer* was first produced there in the fall of 1877.

The opera was well received, and in the same year Gilbert sent Sullivan the libretto of a new work, *H. M. S. Pinafore*.

Sullivan wrote the lighthearted music during an agonizing attack of illness.

Pinafore was produced in 1878. After a slow start, the new opera swept the nation. Pirated versions opened in New York. To protect their interests, Gilbert and Sullivan produced their own authorized version of the work in America.

When their next opera, *The Pirates of Penzance*, was completed, they produced it at the same time in England and the United States, hoping that this would protect their rights in both countries. The plan was only partly successful. Gilbert and Sullivan operas were still pirated in America and other parts of the world.

During the run of Gilbert and Sullivan's *Patience*, which followed *The Pirates*, D'Oyly Carte moved the production from the Opéra Comique to the new theater he had built in London. He called his theater the Savoy because it was located near the historic old Savoy Chapel. Since the theater was planned as a home for Gilbert and Sullivan productions, all the Gilbert and Sullivan works came to be known as the Savoy operas.

The first opera to have its premiere performance in the new theater was *Iolanthe*, in 1882. Six months later Sullivan was knighted by Queen Victoria. His music, as well as his personal charm, had long pleased the royal family. But Gilbert, in his speech and writings, had ridiculed some of Britain's most cherished institutions, and he was not knighted until late in life, after the death of Queen Victoria.

In 1884 a new Gilbert and Sullivan opera, *Princess Ida*, was performed. While the work was being written and rehearsed, there were disagreements between the author and composer. Once *Princess Ida* was launched, Sullivan informed D'Oyly

Carte that he would write no more for the Savoy Theatre. Besides being ill and exhausted, he was weary of light operas. For years he had been told by friends and critics that his talents were being wasted on the music he wrote to Gilbert's librettos. After he was knighted, they even insisted that a collaboration between *Sir* Arthur Sullivan and *Mr*. William Gilbert was hardly proper.

D'Oyly Carte could not believe that Sullivan really meant to break up the successful partnership, nor could Gilbert believe it. They pleaded and argued, until at last Sullivan agreed to set another Gilbert libretto to music. So, in 1885, the greatest popular success of all the Gilbert and Sullivan operas was staged at the Savoy. It was *The Mikado.*

The Mikado was a phenomenon in the theater world. It was played by companies in America, South Africa, Australia, and throughout Europe. Its long run gave Gilbert and Sullivan a two-year breathing spell. Their next opera, *Ruddigore*, did not appear until 1887.

Ruddigore fell far short of the success of *The Mikado*, and Sullivan's advisers were on hand to remind him that, after all, his greatest gift lay in "serious" music.

Sullivan's old illness was troubling him. He and Gilbert quarreled, were reconciled, and quarreled again. But somehow, in the fall of 1888, another Gilbert and Sullivan masterpiece, *The Yeomen of the Guard*, was ready for production.

During the run of *The Yeomen*, Gilbert and Sullivan met to talk over their next work. The queen herself had told Sullivan that he should compose a grand opera. Now he proposed that he and Gilbert turn to something more serious.

Gilbert made a counterproposition—that Sullivan compose comic operas with him and grand operas with someone else. The composer answered that he was weary of comic opera, weary of setting Gilbert's fantastic stories to music.

Their differences led to another quarrel, but before many months they were on friendly terms again and at work on a comic opera, *The Gondoliers*, which was first performed in 1889.

Early in 1890 Gilbert went off to India. When he came home a few weeks later he found that D'Oyly Carte had bought carpets for the Savoy Theatre and charged the cost to the D'Oyly Carte-Gilbert-Sullivan partnership. The partners had agreed to share the expense of the productions, but Gilbert felt that it was unfair to be charged for carpets, especially such expensive ones as D'Oyly Carte had ordered.

He protested. D'Oyly Carte answered sharply. When Sullivan was drawn into the quarrel and sided with D'Oyly Carte, Gilbert declared the partnership dissolved. He brought legal action against the other two and forced a settlement of the expenses. Afterward he admitted he had acted hastily, but Sullivan and D'Oyly Carte could not forget that they had been publicly humiliated.

Sullivan, free of Gilbert and free of the demands of comic opera, had begun what he hoped would be his greatest work. He was composing a grand opera based on Sir Walter Scott's *Ivanhoe*.

D'Oyly Carte built a new theater, the Royal English Opera House, which was to be the home of English grand opera. *Ivanhoe* had its first performance there on January 31, 1891. It was a lavish production, and the public and critics were rapturous in their praise. But after a five-month run, *Ivanhoe* closed, and the Royal English Opera House became the Palace Music Hall.

Both Gilbert and Sullivan tried collaborating with others, but if they had not been happy together, neither were they happy apart. Each seemed to realize he could do his best work only with the other.

Once more they were brought together. Once more they collaborated on a comic opera, *Utopia Limited, or The Flowers of Progress*. D'Oyly Carte produced it at the Savoy Theatre in 1893. *Utopia* had a fairly long run of 245 performances, yet it was not revived for the professional stage until more than half a century later, and it is not widely performed today.

The final Gilbert and Sullivan collaboration was *The Grand Duke, or The Statutory Duel*. It opened at the Savoy in 1896. But the old magic was gone. *The Grand Duke* had only a short run and was never revived.

In 1898 Sullivan conducted a performance of *The Sorcerer*, and he and Gilbert appeared on stage and took a bow together. They never met again. Sullivan died on November 22, 1900.

Gilbert continued to write for the theater. He spent more and more time at Grim's Dyke, his country home near London. On May 29, 1911, he was swimming with friends in the pool on his estate. A girl in the party called for help. Gilbert swam to her aid. The exertion brought on a heart attack. He was dead when he was taken from the pool.

Gilbert had hoped that his fame would rest in his stage dramas. Sullivan had believed he would be remembered for what he considered his serious compositions. Yet it is the "entertainments"—the comic operas they wrote together—that have lived after them, still miraculously fresh, still loved the world over.

Trial by Jury

&§ *After the failure of their first opera,* THESPIS, *Gilbert and Sullivan might never have worked together again if D'Oyly Carte had not asked them for a short piece to fill out a bill at his theater. Gilbert had a libretto on hand. It was* TRIAL BY JURY, *based on a poem he had written for* FUN *magazine seven years before. He read the manuscript to Sullivan. The ridiculousness of the story appealed to Sullivan's sense of humor. Within two weeks he had composed the music.*

TRIAL BY JURY *was first produced at the Royalty Theatre in London on March 25, 1875. It is Gilbert and Sullivan's only one-act opera.*

ả❧ At the hour of ten, barristers, attorneys, and jurymen waited in a court of justice where a trial was about to begin. Angelina, the plaintiff, had charged Edwin, the defendant, with breach of promise.

The usher, who had charge of the courtroom door, admonished the jurymen that they were not to be prejudiced in any way. They had only to look at the face of the brokenhearted plaintiff to sympathize with her distress. As for the defendant, said the usher, "What *he* may say, you needn't mind."

Edwin, the defendant, introduced himself.

The jurymen shook their fists at him and called him a monster.

He begged them not to condemn him without a hearing. At first, he said, he had been happy with Angelina. He had thrown his riches at her feet. He had moped and sighed like a lovesick boy. Then he had grown weary of her and had become the lovesick boy of someone else.

The jurymen conferred among themselves. They admitted that in their youth they, too, had behaved like cads, but now they were respectable. Therefore they hadn't a scrap of sympathy for the defendant.

The judge took his place on the bench. The court hailed him with all the deference due a man of his position.

He announced that before the trial began he wished to tell them how he came to be a judge. As a poor, ambitious barrister, he said, he grew tired of traveling third-class and dining on bread and water, so he fell in love with a rich attorney's elderly, ugly daughter. The grateful father helped him advance in the world. By the time he became wealthy, the elderly, ugly daughter was a hindrance, so he abandoned her.

"Now I'm ready to try the breach of promise of marriage," he said, "for now I am a judge!"

"And a good judge, too!" said the barristers, lawyers, and jurymen.

The counsel for the plaintiff asked that his client be brought in.

The usher called for Angelina. A group of bridesmaids filed in and told the court that the cheated maid was on her way.

The judge took an immediate fancy to the first bridesmaid and sent her a note by the usher. She read it, kissed it rapturously, and placed it in her bosom.

Angelina made her entrance. At once the judge transferred his admiration to her. He ordered the usher to take the note from the first bridesmaid and give it to the plaintiff. The usher obeyed. Angelina read the note, kissed it rapturously, and placed it in *her* bosom.

"Ah, sly dog!" said the jurymen, playfully shaking their fingers at the judge.

He asked them what they thought of the plaintiff. The foreman of the jury had but one word—*rapture*.

The plaintiff curtseyed, quite overcome by their gallantry.

"We love you fondly," said the jury, "and would make you ours."

"Ah, sly dogs!" said the bridesmaids, shaking their fingers at the jurymen.

Angelina's counsel addressed the court. Never, said he, had he known that a man could be so base as to deceive this trusting girl.

The judge noticed Angelina's unsteadiness as she started to the witness stand. The foreman of the jury invited her to recline on him if she were feeling faint, and she fell, sobbing, upon his breast.

"Or if you'd rather," said the judge, "recline on me."

Angelina promptly fell sobbing upon *his* breast.

The jurymen shook their fists at the defendant, again calling him a monster and demanding heavy damages.

When order was restored, Edwin spoke in his own defense.

He had been unfaithful to Angelina, it was true, but only because he obeyed the laws of nature, and nature was constantly changing.

A young fellow was very apt to love this lady today and that lady tomorrow. He proposed, therefore, "If it will appease her sorrow, I'll marry *this* lady today and I'll marry *that* lady tomorrow."

The judge found this reasonable, but Angelina's counsel objected. It was a serious matter, he said, to marry two women at one time.

Angelina threw her arms about Edwin, calling on the court to witness how she adored him. "See what a blessing I've lost, and remember it when you assess the damages Edwin must pay."

He repelled her, shouting that he was always a drunken bully, and that if she married him he would kick her and thrash her and she wouldn't be able to endure him even for a day.

Still she clung to him, until he threw her off and into the arms of her counsel.

The judge concluded that the whole question was one of liquor: "He says when tipsy he would thrash and kick her. Let's make him tipsy, gentlemen, and try."

"I object," said the counsel.

"I don't object," said Edwin.

But all the others raised objections. The trial had reached a deadlock.

In exasperation, the judge threw his books and papers into the air. He was weary of the proceedings and in a hurry to get away, and he offered his final proposal, "I will marry her myself!"

He came down from the bench and took Angelina in his arms.

She was overjoyed. Wealth surrounded her, and all her grief was past.

The counsel was delighted to see the case so favorably decided for his client.

Edwin wondered whether or not this marriage would be a success. The usher pointedly reminded him that His Honor should be the best judge of that.

"Yes, I am a judge," said the judge.

"And a good judge, too!" chorused the others.

The Sorcerer

❧ *In the spring of 1877 Gilbert sent Sullivan the libretto of* THE SORCERER. *Six months later Sullivan had finished the music.* THE SORCERER *was the first opera written under the Gilbert-Sullivan-D'Oyly Carte partnership. It had its premiere performance at the Opéra Comique in London on November 17, 1877.*

ACT I ৯~ Outside Sir Marmaduke Pointdextre's mansion, men and women of Ploverleigh village had met to celebrate the betrothal of Sir Marmaduke's son, Alexis, and Lady Sangazure's daughter, Aline.

The Widow Partlet arrived with her daughter, Constance. Mrs. Partlet was a pew-opener in the village church. Like the other villagers, she was caught up in the spirit of the happy occasion, and she could not understand why her daughter was depressed.

"You alone are sad," she said. "What is the reason?"

Constance refused to answer. Mrs. Partlet sent the others away. Only then did the girl confess that a hopeless love caused her to weep and sigh.

"Who is the object of your young affections?" asked her mother.

"Hush!" said Constance. "He is here!"

Dr. Daly, vicar of Ploverleigh, had appeared.

"To such a union I shall not offer any opposition," said Mrs. Partlet. "Take him—he is yours."

"But Mother," said Constance, "he is not yours to give."

"That's true, indeed," said Mrs. Partlet. "But come—take heart—I'll probe him on the subject."

Dr. Daly, lost in thought, had not even seen them. He was meditating on days long past, when he had been a saintly youth and maidens had adored him.

Mrs. Partlet led her daughter forward. Dr. Daly spoke to

22

them kindly and observed that Constance was quite a little woman.

"She's nearly eighteen," said Mrs. Partlet. "I'm afraid I shall soon lose her."

"You pain me," said Dr. Daly. "Is she delicate?"

"Oh no, sir," said Mrs. Partlet, "but young girls look to get married."

"To be sure," he said. "But there's plenty of time for that. When the time does come, I shall have much pleasure in marrying her myself—"

Constance uttered a cry.

"To some young fellow in her own rank of life," finished the vicar, and the girl burst into tears.

Mrs. Partlet ventured to ask why *he* had never married.

He answered with hollow humor that he had waited too long—he was an old fogy now. "My mind is quite made up," he said. "I shall live and die a solitary old bachelor."

"Oh, Mother!" sobbed Constance, and Mrs. Partlet took her away.

Dr. Daly said to himself, "Poor little girl, I'm afraid she has something on her mind."

Alexis approached with his father, Sir Marmaduke. Dr. Daly congratulated the young man on his coming marriage.

"My dear old tutor and my valued pastor," responded Alexis, "I thank you from the bottom of my heart."

Dr. Daly left father and son alone together. Sir Marmaduke, too, offered his congratulations. Alexis was a fortunate fellow, he said, to be uniting with the house of Sangazure. Aline was not only rich, but she came from a sufficiently old family.

"Father, I am welling over with joy!" said Alexis.

Sir Marmaduke cautioned him that it was not delicate to speak so openly of his love.

"A man who loves as I love—" began Alexis.

"Pooh, pooh, sir!" said Sir Marmaduke. "Fifty years ago I madly loved your future mother-in-law, the Lady Sanga-zure." But, he told his son, *their* conduct had been more delicate—more respectful.

Aline came out upon the terrace, accompanied by a group of girls. Lady Sangazure joined them. She and Sir Marma-duke gazed at each other with signs of strong emotion, which they tried to conceal. Alexis and Aline showed no such reti-cence. They rushed into each other's arms, then withdrew to another part of the terrace.

Sir Marmaduke paid his respects to Lady Sangazure with stately courtesy. Inwardly he was wild with adoration for her.

She replied with calm politeness, concealing the mad fasci-nation she felt for him.

The notary called Alexis and Aline, and they signed the contract that made them legally betrothed.

The others considerately left the couple alone.

Alexis asked, "Are you not very, very happy?" He be-lieved that all the ills of the world could be cured if everyone would break down the false barriers of rank, wealth, educa-tion, age, beauty, and taste and fall in love and marry. "True love should be independent of external influences," he de-clared. "Love should live for love alone."

She praised his noble principles.

"And I am going to take a desperate step in support of them," he said. "Have you ever heard of J. W. Wells and Company, the well-established family sorcerers?"

She answered that she had seen their advertisement.

They had invented a philtre, he told her, which he intended to distribute through the village. As a result, every adult in the place would be blessed with happiness.

Aline was not sure of the meaning of *philtre*. "You don't mean a love potion?"

"I *do* mean a love potion," he said.

He summoned Mr. Wells, who had been resting in his tent nearby. The sorcerer introduced himself as John Wellington Wells, a dealer in magic and spells. The Love-at-First-Sight Philtre, he said, was his company's leading article.

Alexis ordered it in quantity and sent Aline to fetch a teapot.

Mr. Wells described the effects of the philtre. Whoever drank it lost consciousness. Then, when a man awakened, he fell in love with the first lady he met. By the same supernatural law, a lady fell in love with the first man she met.

Aline had fetched a large teapot. Alexis directed the sorcerer to pour enough of the philtre into it to affect the whole village.

Aline reminded him, "Many of the villagers are married people."

Mr. Wells gave her his assurance that the potion had no effect whatever on married people.

Darkness fell. Mr. Wells began a mystical and fearful incantation. He poured the philtre into the teapot, and the voices of sprites, fiends, and demons rose from regions below.

The darkness lifted. Mr. Wells beckoned to the unsuspecting villagers. They gathered about him, ready for the banquet that had been prepared. The teacups were passed around.

Mr. Wells, Alexis, and Aline watched as the tea was being drunk. Dr. Daly did not drink from the large pot. He insisted on tea made to his scientific formula, and Constance brought him a small pot and kettle with which he brewed his own.

The effects of the magic potion were quickly felt. All who had drunk it began to rub their eyes and stagger about. They struggled against the charm, then fell to the ground, where they lay in a deep sleep.

ACT II &ᴥ At midnight Mr. Wells came out onto the terrace, carrying a lantern. Alexis and Aline followed him. Villagers still lay where they had fallen.

It was time for the magic to show its power, said the sorcerer.

"My father is not here!" said Alexis.

"And where is my mother?" asked Aline.

Mr. Wells answered that it did not seem right for a lord and lady to be lying fast asleep outdoors. He had had them carried to their homes and put respectably to bed.

The villagers began to stir. Mr. Wells, Alexis, and Aline stole away.

The men and women stretched, yawned, and sat up. They looked at one another. Two by two, they fell in love.

Constance crossed the terrace, leading the village notary. She was weeping.

"Dear friends," she said, "take pity on my lot." She had long loved the kind and reverend Dr. Daly. Yet a moment ago she had seen this plain old man and now she loved *him* madly. He was ill-tempered, ugly, and four times her age—he was everything she detested—but still she loved him!

Alexis and Aline were watching from the back of the terrace. They saw the villagers depart in loving pairs.

Alexis was positive that good would come even of the ill-matched unions. The miserly wife would check the reckless spending of her extravagant husband. The wealthy husband would shower his penniless bride with gifts. The young, lively girl would cheer her aged husband by singing him comic songs. "But one thing remains to be done," Alexis said. "We must drink the philtre ourselves, that I may be assured of your love forever."

Aline protested. She was not willing for their love to be secured by artificial means.

"My dear Aline," said Alexis, "time works terrible changes. I want to place our love beyond the chance of change."

"It is already far beyond the chance," she said. "Have faith in me, for my love can never change."

"Then you refuse?" he asked.

"I do," she said. "If you cannot trust me, you have no right to love me—no right to be loved *by* me."

"Enough, Aline," he said coldly. To him, her refusal meant only that she wished to be free of him.

Dr. Daly approached. He was puzzled, he told them, by

the number of villagers who had asked him to join them in matrimony. Even Alexis' father, he said, had hinted that he might soon change his condition.

"Oh, Alexis, do you hear that?" said Aline. "Are you not delighted?"

Alexis agreed that a union between her mother and his father would be most gratifying.

But Dr. Daly was melancholy. So much talk of weddings recalled to him the happy days when he, too, might have married.

Sir Marmaduke was coming toward them, not with Lady Sangazure, but with Mrs. Partlet!

Alexis and Aline stared in disbelief.

Sir Marmaduke informed them proudly that his declining days were likely to be comforted by the good Mrs. Partlet.

Alexis responded with false heartiness, "Any wife of yours is a mother of mine," but he whispered to Aline, "It is not quite what I would have wished."

Mrs. Partlet asked Alexis' forgiveness. She was aware that she had no wealth or social position, but at least, she said, she could offer Sir Marmaduke the gift of a loving heart.

She and Sir Marmaduke went into the mansion, accompanied by Alexis and Aline, who were trying hard to make the best of the situation. Dr. Daly gazed sentimentally after them; then he, too, went his way.

Mr. Wells came out onto the terrace. He was agitated, knowing at last that his magic had proved evil. As he looked about him, he saw further proof of the wrong he had done. Another stricken, lovelorn woman was coming toward him.

She was Lady Sangazure. She saw the sorcerer and fixed her eyes on him.

"Oh, horrible!" exclaimed Mr. Wells. "She's going to adore me!"

He implored her to hate him; he listed his worst faults. She loved him all the more.

As a last resort, he pretended that he was engaged to be married. She fled in agony and despair, and Mr. Wells, feeling responsible for her grief, ran after her.

Aline appeared with a flask in her hand. She had decided to obey Alexis' wishes, since she could not bear to be parted from him. She drank the philtre.

Starting off to find Alexis, she met Dr. Daly. He was playing a flute and musing on his loneliness.

He saw her standing there. Suddenly, under the spell of the potion, they were madly in love with each other.

Alexis came in search of Aline. "My only love!" he greeted her. "The philtre—you have tasted it?"

"Yes—yes!" she stammered in confusion.

He tried to embrace her. She drew away. Dr. Daly stepped between them.

Aline asked for Alexis' understanding. It was he who had urged her to drink the potion. She should not be blamed for falling under its enchantment.

But Alexis was furious.

"Come, everyone!" he shouted. Villagers came running, and Alexis prepared to denounce the faithless Aline before them all.

Dr. Daly stopped him. "Be just," he said. "The poor child drank the philtre at your insistence. She hurried off to meet you, but most unhappily she met me instead. Fear nothing from me; I will be no man's rival. I shall quit the country at once."

Alexis was touched. "My excellent old friend!" he said.

Mr. Wells returned, with Lady Sangazure in pursuit. Alexis appealed to him, "What is to be done?"

Mr. Wells replied that there was one means by which the spell might be removed.

"Name it—oh, name it!" cried Alexis.

"Either you or I must yield up his life," said Mr. Wells.

"I am ready," said Alexis.

Aline intervened. "It must not be. Mr. Wells, if he must die so that all may be restored to their old loves, what is to become of me? I should be left with no love to be restored to!"

This was true, admitted Mr. Wells. He asked the others to decide between Alexis and himself.

The decision was unanimous. Mr. Wells was the offender. Therefore, he must die.

"So be it—I submit!" said the sorcerer.

A gong sounded. All the villagers changed partners. Sir Marmaduke left Mrs. Partlet and went to Lady Sangazure. Aline left Dr. Daly and went to Alexis. Dr. Daly went to Constance. The old notary left Constance and went to Mrs. Partlet.

Sir Marmaduke invited them all into his mansion for a feast. While the others danced and sang, the sorcerer sank into the earth, with smoke and flames rising about him.

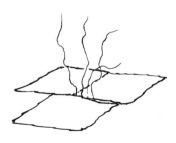

H. M. S. Pinafore

or

THE LASS THAT LOVED A SAILOR

᪍ *Some of the lyrics in* H. M. S. PINAFORE *were taken from Gilbert's* BAB BALLADS. *The story caricatured at least one political figure of the day and was a satire on blind patriotism and the social caste system.*

PINAFORE *opened at the Opéra Comique on May 25, 1878. Audiences were small at first because of a heat wave in London, but after a few weeks the opera was a solid success— one of the greatest successes of all the Gilbert and Sullivan works.*

ACT I ❧ *Her Majesty's Ship Pinafore* lay anchored at Portsmouth. Sailors were busy on the quarterdeck, splicing rope and cleaning brasswork. A woman came aboard with a large basket on her arm. She worked on one of the bumboats that carried provisions to the ships in the harbor. Little Buttercup she was called, although she could never tell why, since she was far from little and not particularly flowerlike.

The boatswain, however, thought her well named, and he pronounced her a rosy, round, red beauty.

"Red, am I?" said Buttercup dourly. "And round and rosy? Maybe, but have you ever thought that beneath a gay and frivolous exterior there may lurk a cankerworm which is slowly but surely eating its way into one's very heart?"

"No, my lass," said the boatswain, "I can't say I've ever thought of that."

A hollow voice spoke up. "*I* have thought of it often!" A sailor came pushing his way through the others, who shrank from him.

"Don't take no heed of *him*," said the boatswain. "That's only poor Dick Deadeye."

Dick was misshapen and ill-mannered. The rest of the crew detested him.

Looking down the hatchway, Buttercup saw a seaman of a more engaging sort. She asked who he might be.

"That is the smartest lad in all the fleet," said the boatswain, "—Ralph Rackstraw!"

"Ha! That name!" said the bumboat woman to herself. "Remorse! Remorse!"

Ralph came up the hatchway. He was a sorrowful man, a lowly-born sailor, hopelessly in love with the captain's daughter.

"Ah, my poor lad, you've climbed too high," said the boatswain. "Our worthy captain's child won't have nothing to say to a poor chap like you. Will she, lads?"

"No, no!" responded the other sailors.

Captain Corcoran came smartly on deck. He and the crew exchanged compliments, and he touched on his own excellent qualities as a sea captain. First, he was never sick at sea, and second, he was never guilty of using profane language.

"What, never?" asked his men.

"No, never," he said.

"What, *never?*" they persisted.

And the captain, hedging slightly, answered, "Hardly ever."

The sailors went below. As soon as they were gone, a look of sorrow crossed the captain's face.

"Sir, you are sad," said Little Buttercup.

Captain Corcoran confided that his daughter, Josephine, was being sought in marriage by Sir Joseph Porter, First Lord of the Admiralty, but strangely she was cool to his attentions.

"Poor Sir Joseph!" sighed Buttercup. "I know too well the anguish of a heart that loves but vainly."

She left him, and the captain said to himself, "A plump and pleasing person!"

Josephine came on deck. Her father was grieved at her melancholy appearance. He had hoped she would look her best today, since Sir Joseph Porter would soon be here to claim her hand.

"Sir Joseph is a great and good man, but oh, I cannot love him!" said Josephine. "My heart is already given."

"Given? And to whom?" demanded her father.

"He is but a humble sailor on board your own ship," she said.

The captain was shocked. "A common sailor? Oh, fie!"

"I blush for my weakness," said Josephine. "I hate myself when I think of the depth to which I have stooped—but I love him."

"My child, let us talk this over," said the captain. He had no doubt that such a man might be brave and worthy, but a common sailor would be out of place in the society to which she was accustomed.

"I have thought of that," she said. "I have a heart; therefore I love. But I am your daughter; therefore I am proud. Though I carry my love with me to the tomb, he shall never know it."

Meanwhile Sir Joseph's barge was nearing the *Pinafore*. Josephine retired to compose herself. The crew came on deck to receive Sir Joseph and the sisters, cousins, and aunts who accompanied him wherever he went.

The female relatives boarded the ship. The sailors welcomed them. Then they all joined in greeting Sir Joseph, who came aboard with his Cousin Hebe on his arm.

Sir Joseph introduced himself as the monarch of the sea, and he outlined the steps by which he had attained his position. He had risen from office boy to a junior partnership in an attorney's firm. There he had grown so rich that he was sent to Parliament. Because he always voted at his party's call and never thought for himself at all, he was made ruler of the Queen's Navy. His Golden Rule for success was, "Stick close to your desks and never go to sea, and you *all* may be rulers of the Queen's Navy."

He cautioned Captain Corcoran that he must always be kind to his crew, because the noble fellows were the bulwark of English greatness. He called Ralph forward. "Can you sing?" he asked.

Ralph replied that he could hum a little.

"Then hum this at your leisure," said Sir Joseph, handing him a sheet of music. "It is a song I have composed for the use of the Royal Navy. It is designed to encourage independence of thought and action in the lower branches of the service and to teach the principle that a British sailor is any man's equal—excepting mine." He turned to the captain. "Now a word with you on a tender and sentimental subject."

Captain Corcoran went below. Sir Joseph followed, taking his relatives with him.

The boatswain observed that Sir Joseph was a true gentleman, courteous and considerate to the very humblest.

"We are not the very humblest," said Ralph. "Sir Joseph has explained our true position to us. He says a British seaman is any man's equal, excepting his."

"You're on the wrong tack," argued Dick Deadeye. "When people have to obey other people's orders, equality is out of the question."

But Ralph stood firm. "I'll speak to the captain's daughter and tell her all the love I have for her. Do you approve of my determination?"

Only Dick expressed disapproval.

The boatswain proposed that they sing Sir Joseph's song to put the miserable Dick Deadeye in a proper state of mind.

They sang the composition, a rousing song in praise of the British sailor. Then they all left, except Ralph, who remained behind, deep in thought.

Josephine came on deck. She, too, was deep in thought. She had just met with Sir Joseph. She knew he was truly a great, good man—for he had told her so himself—yet she could not endure his attentions.

She saw Ralph. Overcome by emotion, she spoke his name.

"Aye, lady," he said. "No other than poor Ralph Rackstraw."

"And why poor?" she asked.

He was poor in happiness, he told her. For six weary months he had been torn by anxiety and doubt. "Josephine," he said, "I am a British sailor, and I love you."

"Sir, this audacity!" she exclaimed, while to herself she was saying, "Oh, my heart, my beating heart!"

"I cannot stoop to implore," he said proudly. "I have spoken, and I wait your word."

"You shall not wait long," she said. "Your love I reject. Go and cast your eyes on some village maiden of your own poor rank."

She swept away.

Ralph's messmates gathered about him, along with Cousin Hebe and the rest of Sir Joseph's female relatives. "What cheer? What did she say?" they asked.

"She rejected my humble gift," he said.

"Oho, I told you so!" croaked Dick Deadeye.

Ralph had resolved to end his life, and he left a message for Josephine. "Tell the maid I loved her well."

His friends wept. The boatswain handed Ralph a loaded pistol.

Suddenly Josephine appeared. She saw Ralph with the weapon at his head. "Stay your hand!" she cried. "I love you!"

"She loves you!" exclaimed the others.

It was a time of ecstatic happiness for the two lovers and their friends. They planned an elopement, which would take place that night. Josephine and Ralph would go ashore. A

clergyman would perform the marriage ceremony, and once they were married, no one could ever part them.

Dick Deadeye tried to warn them against carrying out such a scheme. The others drove him away; then they continued their celebration by singing Sir Joseph's song.

ACT II &❧ It was night. Captain Corcoran was sitting on deck, singing and accompanying himself on a mandolin. His song dealt with his own particular trials—a rebellious crew, a daughter who loved a common sailor, and an angry Sir Joseph.

Little Buttercup was nearby. He gently reproved her for not having gone ashore at dusk.

She had been waiting, she said, hoping to see him smile before she left.

The captain feared it would be a long time before he was cheerful again. "Misfortunes crowd upon me, and all my old friends seem to have turned against me."

"Do not say 'all,' dear captain," she replied.

He thanked her for her regard. "Were we differently situated, I think I could have returned it."

"I understand. You hold aloof from me because you are rich and lofty and I am poor and lowly. But take care," she said warningly. "The poor bumboat woman has gypsy blood in her veins, and she can read destinies." She predicted a change for him. Turning moody and strange, she began to quote familiar maxims in a tone that hinted at some dark mystery. Then, when he was thoroughly bewildered, she left him.

Sir Joseph sought out Captain Corcoran and complained of Josephine's indifference. The captain suggested that she might be overwhelmed by Sir Joseph's high rank.

Josephine came out of her cabin. She was trembling, fearful of the step she was about to take. She pictured her lovely ancestral home and contrasted it with the dingy room in which she might live as a common sailor's wife. Which should she obey—the god of reason or the god of love?

Sir Joseph addressed her. "Madam, it has been represented to me that you are appalled by my exalted rank." If this were true, he assured her that she need not hesitate. It was his opinion that married happiness had nothing to do with difference in rank.

Josephine brightened. "I thank you. I did hesitate, but now I will hesitate no longer."

Sir Joseph was triumphant, not suspecting how well he had pleaded his rival's cause.

He and the captain rejoiced in what they took to be Josephine's acceptance of Sir Joseph's offer. Josephine, too, rejoiced. Now, at last, she felt free to follow her heart.

She and Sir Joseph went below.

Dick Deadeye found Captain Corcoran alone. "I've come to give you warning," he said furtively, and he revealed the plans for Josephine's and Ralph's elopement.

"Dick Deadeye, I thank you," said the captain. "I will at once take means to arrest their flight." He produced a cat-o'-nine-tails, with which unruly sailors were flogged. He wrapped himself in a cloak that concealed his face. Dick Deadeye gloated, "They are foiled—foiled—foiled!"

Crewmen began to gather on deck. Ralph and the boatswain met Josephine, who had just come out of her cabin with Little Buttercup. As they were starting away, the captain stamped on the deck. The conspirators asked in alarm, "Why, what was that?"

Dick said, "It was the cat."

The conspirators were reassured. "It was," they said, "it was the cat."

"They're right," said the captain grimly, flourishing the cat-o'-nine-tails. "It *was* the cat."

He threw off his disguise.

Ralph and Josephine defied him. The lowly sailor had raised his eyes above the dust, they declared. Now he dared assert himself as an Englishman.

"He is an Englishman!" said the crew.

"He is an Englishman!" repeated the boatswain. "In spite of all temptations to belong to other nations, he remains an Englishman!"

These noble sentiments did nothing to relieve the captain's anger. He did not wish to speak slightingly of any British seaman, he said, "but when you seek your captain's child in marriage, why damme, it's too bad!"

Cousin Hebe and Sir Joseph's other female relatives had come on deck in time to hear the captain's outburst. Sir Joseph, too, had come on deck.

"Did you hear him?" said Cousin Hebe in shocked tones. "He is swearing—he is swearing!"

Sir Joseph was amazed and distressed at the language he had heard. He ordered Captain Corcoran away.

The captain retired in disgrace. Sir Joseph spoke kindly to Ralph. "Tell me, my fine fellow, how came your captain to forget himself? I am quite sure you had given him no cause for annoyance."

Before Ralph could answer, Josephine threw herself into his arms.

"She is the figurehead of my ship of life," he said, "the bright beacon that guides me into my port of happiness."

Sir Joseph was outraged. "Insolent fellow!" he shouted. "Seize him!"

Two sailors seized Ralph and handcuffed him.

Josephine pleaded for him. Ignoring her, Sir Joseph ordered Ralph loaded with chains and thrown into the ship's dungeon.

The two lovers bade each other a tearful farewell, and Ralph was dragged away.

Little Buttercup had been waiting to speak. The time had come, she said, for her to confess a long-hidden crime. Many years ago she had practiced baby-farming. In the course of her career she had cared for two babies—one lowly born, the other of high estate. Her crime was that she had mixed the children up. The well-born babe was Ralph Rackstraw; the other was Captain Corcoran!

Sir Joseph asked, "Am I to understand that Ralph is really the captain and the captain is Ralph?"

"That is the idea I intended to convey," replied Buttercup.

"Dear me!" said Sir Joseph. "Let them appear at once."

Ralph and the captain were brought before him. Already Ralph was dressed as the captain, and the captain wore a seaman's uniform.

Now that this change had taken place, said Sir Joseph, his marriage with Josephine would be out of the question.

"Don't say that," said the former captain. "Love levels all ranks."

"It does not level them as much as that," said Sir Joseph. He handed Josephine over to Ralph. "Here, take her, sir."

The two lovers embraced.

So that Sir Joseph would not be left alone, Cousin Hebe promised to comfort his declining days. The former captain, now a man of humble rank, was free to wed Buttercup. In the words of Sir Joseph, "Tomorrow morn our vows shall all be plighted; three loving pairs on the same day united!"

The Pirates of Penzance

or

THE SLAVE OF DUTY

⮾ *Gilbert and Sullivan were in America for the opening of* THE PIRATES OF PENZANCE—*at the Fifth Avenue Theatre in New York on December 31, 1879. The opera had already been given on December 30 in Paignton, England, but this was only a token performance, with the performers reading from the manuscript. By presenting* THE PIRATES *at the same time in the United States and England, Gilbert and Sullivan helped protect their rights in both countries.*

The first full-scale English production was at the Opéra Comique in London on April 3, 1880.

49

A C T I 𝒮 On the coast of Cornwall, near the town of Penzance, a band of pirates had assembled to celebrate a special occasion. Frederic, their apprentice, had just come of age, and his term of apprenticeship was ending. From this day on, he would rank as a full-fledged pirate.

The king and the other pirates offered the young man their good wishes.

Frederic was sorry he could not repay them as they deserved. "Today," he said, "I leave you forever."

The king was incredulous. How could Frederic think of leaving when he had learned his trade so well?

"Yes, I have done my best for you," said the young man, "and why? It was my duty, and I am the slave of duty. As a child, I was apprenticed to your band through an error—no matter. The mistake was not yours, and I was honor-bound by it."

Samuel, the pirate lieutenant, asked what mistake had been made. Frederic refused to tell, since it would reflect on his beloved Ruth, the pirate maid-of-all-work.

Ruth had overheard Frederic's gallant speech, and she asked that she be shielded no longer.

When Frederic was small, she told the pirates, he was so adventurous that his father thought he should have a seafaring career. She was the boy's nurserymaid, and Frederic's father asked her to take the boy and apprentice him to a pilot. But she had misunderstood the word and apprenticed him to a *pirate*.

After this disaster, she dared not go back to the boy's father. She attached herself to the pirate crew so that she might still be near her former charge.

She begged Frederic's forgiveness.

He had long ago pardoned her, he said. He addressed the pirates, saying that singly he loved them all, but as a group he detested them utterly and felt bound to devote himself to destroying them.

The king agreed that a man should always be guided by his conscience.

"Besides," added Samuel, "we can offer you but little temptation to remain with us. We don't seem to make piracy pay. I don't know why, but we don't."

"*I* know why," said Frederic, "but I mustn't tell you. It wouldn't be right."

The king and Samuel pressed him to tell them, reminding him that it was only half-past eleven and he was still one of them until the clock struck twelve.

"Well, then, it is my duty as a pirate to tell you that you are too tenderhearted," said Frederic. The pirates never attacked a weaker party than themselves, and when they attacked a stronger party they were always beaten. Besides, they made it a point never to harm an orphan.

"Of course," said Samuel. "We are orphans ourselves."

"Yes, but it has got about," Frederic told them. "Now everyone we capture says he is an orphan."

Samuel defended their position. "You wouldn't have us absolutely merciless?"

"Until twelve o'clock I would," said Frederic. "After twelve I wouldn't."

"And Ruth—whom you love so well and who has won her middle-aged way into your heart—what is to become of her?" the maid-of-all-work asked piteously.

Frederic was not sure. He was beginning to have doubts about taking her with him when he left the pirates. He had been constantly at sea since he was eight years old, and in all that time she was the only woman he had seen. Since he was not able to compare her with other women, she might be less attractive than he thought, and it would be a terrible thing to marry her and discover that she was plain.

The pirates went to their ship. Ruth stayed, trying to persuade Frederic not to leave her. As for her appearance, she insisted that she was still a fine woman.

"Thank you, Ruth. I believe you," he said.

They heard the sound of voices.

"Confusion! The voices of young girls!" said Ruth to herself. "If he should see them, I am lost!"

Frederic had already seen them climbing over the rocks. They were lovely—each one graceful, delicate, and refined. And Ruth had told him *she* was beautiful!

"You have deceived me!" he said, and she fled.

Not wishing to be seen in his pirate garb, Frederic hid in a cave as the girls came in sight.

They were sisters on a holiday.

"What a picturesque spot!" said the girl called Kate.

"I wonder where papa is," said the one called Edith.

"Oh, he will be here presently," said the one called Isabel.

"We are quite alone," said Edith, "and the sea is smooth. Suppose we take off our shoes and stockings and paddle."

Each had taken off one shoe when Frederic stepped out of the cave. He had not intended to intrude, he said, but under the circumstances he felt duty-bound to let them know they were being observed.

"Who are you, sir?" asked Edith.

"I am a pirate," he answered.

The girls were horrified.

He prayed that they would not shun him. Was there not one, he asked, who, with her affection, would help rescue him from his unfortunate position?

"No," they said.

"Not one?" he asked.

"Yes, one!" said a voice. It was the voice of Mabel, another sister, who had just overtaken the others.

She chided her sisters. Were they all deaf to pity? She freely offered Frederic her love if it would help him find true peace of mind.

The other girls stood by, talking animatedly about the weather, while they listened to everything Frederic and their sister were saying.

He suddenly remembered that the pirates were due back at any moment. He warned the young ladies that they should leave.

He and Mabel were able to get away, but before the others could escape, the pirates surrounded them. Each man seized a girl. The king seized two.

The men were delighted with their prizes. They remembered that there was a minister in the neighborhood who could quickly marry them to their captives.

Mabel returned. "Hold, monsters!" she cried. "Before you proceed to wed us against our will, bear in mind that Father is a major-general!"

The pirates hesitated.

"Yes, yes," said the girls, "he is a major-general!"

Meanwhile their father, General Stanley, had come unnoticed into the pirates' lair. "Yes," he said, hearing himself mentioned, "I am a major-general."

After he had told them of the glories of his position and the vastness of his knowledge, he asked what was going on.

"We propose to marry your daughters," said Samuel.

"Against our wills, papa, against our wills," said the girls.

"Oh, but you mustn't do that," said the general. Looking at the men's uniforms, he asked, "Who are you?"

"They are pirates," said Edith, "the famous pirates of Penzance."

"All except this gentleman," said Mabel, indicating Frederic.

"I object to pirates as sons-in-law," said the general.

The king replied that the pirates objected to major-generals as fathers-in-law but were willing to overlook the point.

The general had heard of the pirates of Penzance and their tender concern for orphans. He appealed to their sympathies. Would they rob him of his daughters and leave him to pass the rest of his life alone? Did they know what it was to be an orphan?

"Oh, dash it all!" said the pirates in disgust, and the king said, "Here we are again."

The general said pathetically, "Have pity on my lonely state. I am an orphan boy."

The king weighed the situation and decided that the major-general and his daughters were free to go.

The pirates were happy with their romantic adventure, even though it had ended short of marriage. They began to dance. The major-general waved a British flag. The pirates produced their own black flag with its skull and crossbones. Ruth had come back to make a last appeal to Frederic, and he cast her from him.

ACT II 🙠 In a ruined, moonlit chapel General Stanley sat, surrounded by his daughters. He was weeping, and they tried in vain to comfort him.

Frederic entered, and Mabel asked if he could say something to relieve her father's sorrow.

"I will try," said Frederic, "but why does he sit, night after night, in this drafty old ruin?"

The general answered him. "To escape the pirates' clutches, I described myself as an orphan, and heaven help me, I am no orphan. I come here to humble myself before the tombs of my ancestors and to implore their pardon for having brought them dishonor."

To Frederic this was absurd. The general had bought the property only a year ago. The ancestors buried here were not *his* ancestors.

But to the general, they *were* his ancestors, since he owned their tombs.

Frederic tried to console him. "Had you not acted as you did, those reckless men would have married your large family on the spot."

Still General Stanley felt deep remorse. He would have gone to the pirates and confessed his sin, he said, if he had not been afraid they might harm him. He asked Frederic, "At what time does your expedition march against them?"

At eleven, replied Frederic, and by midnight he hoped to have swept the pirates off the face of the earth. Then he would feel free to claim Mabel as his own.

He had called on the local police for help. The policemen, led by their sergeant, marched into the chapel. The sergeant confessed that they were not always the bravest of men and sometimes they had to keep up their courage by slapping their chests and imitating the stirring sounds of a trumpet.

Mabel and her sisters urged them on to battle — "Go, ye heroes, go to glory! Go, ye heroes, go and die!"

The policemen had had no thought of dying on the field of glory. The idea left them highly nervous, although they tried to put on a brave front to suit the occasion.

"Away, away!" said General Stanley.

"We go," said the men.

"Yes, but you *don't* go!" said the general.

And at last the sergeant led his reluctant men away. Mabel tore herself from Frederic's arms and left the chapel, followed by her sisters and the general.

Before Frederic could join the policemen, two figures leaped in through the window, flourishing pistols. They were Ruth and the pirate king.

Frederic asked how they dared face him. Did they not know that he had sworn to exterminate them?

But in spite of their drawn pistols, the visitors seemed friendly enough. Knowing Frederic's taste for puzzles and curiosities, they said, they had brought him word of a paradox.

Frederic was interested.

Long ago, said the king, it had been decided that February was to have only twenty-eight days, except once in four years, when it would have one day more. Frederic had been born in a leap-year, on the twenty-ninth of February. "Though you've lived twenty-one years," said the pirate king, "if we go by birthdays, you're only five years old!"

They all laughed heartily at this paradox.

"You are glad now, I'll be bound, that you spared us," said Ruth. "You would never have forgiven yourself when you discovered that you had killed two of your comrades."

"My *comrades?*" said Frederic.

The king made the point clear. Frederic had been apprenticed to the pirates, not until he reached his twenty-first year, but until he reached his twenty-first *birthday*. According to birthdays, he was only five.

Frederic quailed. Surely, he said, they were not going to hold him to that.

"We merely remind you," said the king, "and leave the rest to your sense of duty."

Frederic shuddered at the thought of ever having been associated with the pirates, yet his duty came before all else. "At any price," he said, "I will do my duty."

"Bravely spoken," said the king. "Come, you are one of us once more."

Now that Frederic was again an apprentice pirate, his duty forced him to reveal how General Stanley had deceived them by pretending to be an orphan.

The enraged king vowed revenge. He and Ruth went to gather the pirates for an attack on the general.

Mabel entered and found Frederic reduced to tears. He told her of the terrible paradox that bound him to the pirates for sixteen more leap years, and he bade her farewell. In some sixty-four years, he said, he would come back to claim her hand.

"It seems so long," she said.

"Swear you will be true to me," he said.

"Yes, I will be strong," she promised, and he sprang out through the window.

The policemen marched back into the chapel. Mabel sadly informed them that Frederic could no longer lead them to death and glory because he was once more a pirate.

This was shameful, said the policemen.

"You know nothing about it. He has done his duty," said Mabel loftily, and she left them.

The policemen made ready to move against the enemy without Frederic's help, although they actually disliked arresting their fellow citizens and depriving them of their freedom. All in all, they concluded, a policeman's lot was not a happy one.

The pirates advanced. They were not coming for gold, they said, but to avenge themselves on the deceitful major-general.

The police hid as the pirates came in through the ruined windows of the chapel. The king, Frederic, and Ruth were with them.

"Hush, not a word," said Frederic. "The major-general comes." The pirates concealed themselves.

The major-general entered, wearing a dressing gown and carrying a light. Tormented by guilt, he had not been able to sleep. His daughters came into the chapel to find out why he had left his bed at such a late hour.

The pirates came out of concealment. The king ordered his men to seize the major-general.

The police rose from their hiding places. There was a fierce struggle, which ended with the police on the floor and the pirates standing over them.

The police sergeant admitted defeat, but, he said, the pirates would not triumph for long.

The king said menacingly, "Don't say you are orphans, for we know that game."

"We've a stronger claim," said the sergeant. "We charge you to yield in Queen Victoria's name!"

"You do?" said the king, baffled.

"We do," said the police.

The pirates fell to their knees. "We yield at once," said the king, "because, with all our faults, we love our queen."

Ruth faced the police and the major-general. "One moment! Let me tell you who they are." These pirates were no members of the common throng, she said. All were noblemen, British peers who had gone wrong!

This fact altered the entire situation. "With all our faults," said the general, "we love our House of Peers."

He addressed his former enemies, "I pray you pardon me. Peers will be peers, and youth will have its fling. Resume your ranks and legislative duties, and take my daughters, all of whom are beauties!"

Patience

or

BUNTHORNE'S BRIDE

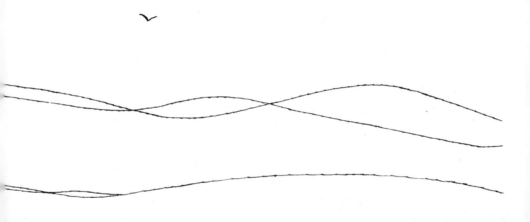

About 1880 London was caught up in an "aesthetic" craze. Young men wore long hair and knee breeches, and girls dressed in flowing robes. They wrote poetry, idolized their favorite poets, and met for discussions of High Art. Gilbert caricatured the "aesthetes" in his story of PATIENCE. The opera was first performed at the Opéra Comique in London on April 23, 1881.

A C T I ❧ Twenty lovesick maidens lingered outside Bunthorne Castle. Three of them—Ella, Angela, and Saphir—led the others in a despairing song. All loved Reginald Bunthorne, master of the castle, and their hopeless love bound them together in a forlorn sisterhood.

Bunthorne looked on them with cold indifference. They had long believed that because he was a poet and lived in a world of poetic fancy, love meant nothing to him. But this was not the case, asserted Lady Jane, one of the maidens. She had just discovered that Bunthorne was wildly in love with Patience, the village milkmaid.

Patience came in sight on a rocky hill near the castle. She looked with pity on the despondent maidens.

Saphir spoke to her. "Happy girl—loved by a poet!"

Angela asked, "Is it true that you have never loved?"

"Most true," answered Patience.

To the maidens this was strange and deplorable. The milkmaid pointed out that she was never sad, while they sat weeping and sighing. Still they insisted that if she had never loved, she had never known true happiness. They started off to sing their morning carol outside Bunthorne's door.

"Stay," said Patience. "I have some news for you. The Thirty-fifth Dragoon Guards have halted in the village and are on their way to this very spot."

"We care nothing for dragoon guards," said Ella.

"Bless me!" said Patience. "You were all engaged to them a year ago."

"My poor child, you don't understand these things," said Angela, and the maidens moved off together, singing mournfully. Patience looked after them in puzzlement. Then she, too, went away.

The officers of the dragoon guard appeared, in dashing red and yellow uniforms. They took great pride in being soldiers of the queen; according to the colonel, a dragoon was indeed a remarkable man.

The Duke of Dunstable, a lieutenant in the guard, came listlessly forward. He was a gloomy sort of fellow. Because of his wealth and rank, he had known nothing but flattery, and such a life had wearied him. He had joined the army, where he might be snubbed or even bullied, and he looked on this as a welcome change.

Meanwhile Bunthorne had come out of his castle. The maidens followed him, playing on harps and singing. He was absorbed in the poem he was composing, and they were absorbed in him.

The officers were indignant to think that their former sweethearts preferred this melancholy literary man to them. The major asked the maidens what in the world had come over them.

"Bunthorne!" said Lady Jane. "*He* has come over us!"

The poet was still in the agonies of composition. At last he found the word he had been seeking. He wrote it down.

"At last! Finished!" he gasped.

Patience had come back. He caught her hand.

The maidens were asking him to read what he had written. It was wild and weird, very tender and very yearning, he told them. It was called, "Oh, Hollow, Hollow, Hollow."

He recited his composition. Choked with emotion, he hurried away.

His poem left the maidens in a state of rapture.

"It seemed to me to be nonsense," said Patience.

The colonel broke in. "This is all very well," he said to the maidens, "but you seem to forget that you are engaged to us."

"It can never be," said Saphir.

Lady Jane looked with scorn at the red and yellow of

the men's uniforms. "Come, maidens," she said, and they followed her away.

The affronted dragoons marched off angrily.

Bunthorne returned. Now that he was alone and unobserved, his manner changed. He dropped his aesthetic pose and admitted that he was a sham. His drab costumes, his elegant mannerisms, his poetic fancies—all were pretense born of a love of admiration.

He saw Patience and called her to him. Did she ever yearn? he asked. Did she know what it was to seek oceans and find puddles?

The strange words alarmed her.

"Don't be frightened," he said. "It's only poetry."

"Then I don't like poetry," said the girl.

"Don't you?" he said eagerly, and he confessed that he did not like poetry either. "Patience, I have long loved you," he said. He promised to cut his hair and become frolicsome if it would please her.

She stopped him. She knew nothing of love, she said, but she was quite certain that she could never love him.

Crushed by her refusal, he staggered away.

She was bewildered and disturbed. Angela came by and asked her what was the matter.

Patience begged her to explain this love that was so upsetting to everyone.

"Poor, blind child!" said Angela. She explained that love was pure and refined—the one emotion that was truly unselfish.

Patience wept. To think that she had lived all these years without having known this unselfish emotion! What a wicked girl she must be!

"Is it possible that you never loved anybody?" asked Angela.

Patience recalled that once she had loved someone. When she was four she had loved a baby a year older than herself, but she was sure that this did not count, because he was a *little* boy.

After Angela had gone, Patience saw the matter in a different light. Now that she knew love was a duty, she was determined to fall in love at the first opportunity.

A young man came in sight. He stopped, looking into her face. With amazing suddenness he asked her to marry him.

She answered that she did not know him.

"Patience," he said, "have you forgotten the friend of your youth?"

She recognized him then. He was Archibald Grosvenor, whom she had loved as a little boy.

"How you've improved!" she said.

"Yes, I am very beautiful," he said gloomily.

"Surely that doesn't make you unhappy," she said.

"Yes," he replied, "I am completely miserable." It was his terrible destiny to be loved at first sight by every woman he met.

She suggested that he disguise himself.

"That may not be," he told her. "These gifts were given to me for the enjoyment of my fellow creatures."

"You, too, are a poet?" she asked.

He was a poet, he answered, and he was known as Archibald the All-Right.

Patience asked if he could possibly care for such a girl as she.

He gave her his word that he had loved her for full fifteen years.

Patience was in a trance. "We will never, never part," she said.

"We will live and die together," said Grosvenor.

For a moment or two they were gloriously happy. Then Patience realized she must not love him. Love was unselfish, and it would be an act of pure selfishness to take him from all the other women who adored him.

He was forced to accept her logic.

A new thought occurred to her. "Although I may not love you—for you are perfection—there is nothing to prevent your loving *me*. I am plain, homely, unattractive."

"That's true," he agreed.

But this conclusion brought them only sorrow, and they went their separate ways.

Bunthorne returned, surrounded by the maidens. They had crowned him with roses and were dancing ecstatically. Bunthorne's lawyer had joined the party. The dragoons appeared and stared at the odd procession.

Bunthorne announced that Patience had broken his heart and so, on the advice of his lawyer, he was offering himself in a public raffle. He began to hawk the raffle tickets. "Put in half a guinea and you may gain a husband. Put in half a guinea and you may draw him in a lottery. Such an opportunity may not occur again!"

The maidens crowded about him, buying tickets. Lady Jane presented herself.

"Are *you* going to buy a ticket?" he asked.

"Certainly," she said. "Why shouldn't I?"

The lottery tickets were put into a bag. Lady Jane was

selected to draw the winning number. But as she reached into the bag, Patience rushed forward.

"Stay your hand!" she cried. With her newfound understanding of love, she had come to seek Bunthorne's pardon and offer herself as his bride.

The maidens were indignant and called her a bold-faced thing.

But Bunthorne was overjoyed, believing she had loved him all the time and had only been afraid to speak.

"No, Mr. Bunthorne, you're wrong again," she said. In marrying him, she would have no thought of joy or gain. She would only be devoting herself to him in complete unselfishness.

Even under these terms, Bunthorne was happy to claim her as his bride.

The maidens were downcast, but not for long. They began to gaze fondly at the officers, who gazed fondly back. Soon each maiden was reunited with her last year's sweetheart.

Archibald Grosvenor came slowly into sight. He took no notice of anything except the book he was reading.

The maidens watched him with a strange fascination. Gradually they moved away from the dragoons. "Who is this?" they asked.

He looked up from his book to tell them he was a broken-hearted and aesthetic troubadour.

"Then," said the maidens, "we love you!" and they knelt before him.

"They love him! Horror!" said the dragoons. Patience and the jealous Bunthorne echoed the words.

"They love me!" said Grosvenor. "Horror! Horror! Horror!"

ACT II ❧ Lady Jane was alone in a glade in the woods. Leaning on a cello, she listened to the voices of the maidens, who were singing in the distance. "Fools!" she said to herself. They had deserted Bunthorne because he fancied a milkmaid, but she knew in her heart that he would soon grow weary of this fancy. "Then I," she said, "who alone am faithful to him, shall reap my reward." But she realized her charms were fading, and she prayed that Bunthorne would not delay too long.

Accompanying herself on the cello, she sang a song that told of a woman's sadness when she sees her beauties disappear.

After she was gone, Grosvenor came through the woods. The maidens followed him, as they had once followed Bunthorne. He was reading a book and paying no attention to them. When he sat down, they clustered about him and asked him to read to them. Wearily he obliged and read two of his poems, which they admired extravagantly. He was bored by their praise.

"Ladies," he said, "this is Saturday, and you have been following me about since Monday. I should like the usual half-holiday."

"Do not send us away from you," pleaded Saphir.

"It is hard to speak plainly," he said. "I know I am loved by you, but I never can love you in return." To illustrate his point, he told them the fable of the magnet and the churn—of the magnet that turned away from iron and set his love on a silver churn. The story ended with a moral: "By no endeavor can a magnet ever attract a silver churn."

Reluctantly the maidens left him.

Patience came in search of him. She asked if he still loved her as fondly as ever.

"Love you!" he exclaimed, seizing her hand.

She drew herself up indignantly. "If you are a gentleman," she said, "pray remember that I am another's." She added very tenderly, "But you do love me, don't you?"

"Madly, hopelessly, despairingly!" he said.

"That's right," she said. "I can never be yours; but that's right."

He asked if she really loved Bunthorne.

She answered that she was miserable with Bunthorne, but she loved him because it was her duty.

"That's right," said Grosvenor. "I can never be yours; but that's right."

Sorrowfully he left her. She began to weep.

Bunthorne found her there. Lady Jane had followed him. He asked Patience why she was crying.

"I've only been thinking how dearly I love you," she said.

"Love me? Bah!" he said scornfully.

"Love him? Bah!" said Lady Jane.

"Don't interfere," said Bunthorne, and she complained mournfully, "He always crushes me."

Bunthorne all but accused Patience of being in love with Grosvenor.

"You can't love two people at once," she replied.

"I don't believe you know what love is," he said.

"Yes, I do," said Patience. "There was a happy time when I didn't, but bitter experience has taught me." She gave him her own definition of love—a sad song sung by a suffering maid.

Still weeping, she went away.

Bunthorne reflected that everything had gone wrong with him since Grosvenor crossed his path. He resolved to meet his smug-faced rival on his own ground and defeat him. Lady Jane approved Bunthorne's resolution and promised to help him. They left together.

The duke, the colonel, and the major appeared, walking stiffly and self-consciously. They had exchanged their military uniforms for costumes similar to Bunthorne's. They wore long wigs and carried themselves in grotesque and angular attitudes. Their idea was to become as aesthetic as the maidens were, in the hope of winning them back.

Coming through the woods, Angela and Saphir saw the men and were deeply impressed by the change. They condescended to dance with the budding aesthetes, and at last all five danced off together.

Grosvenor returned to the glade with a mirror in his hand. He found it pleasant to be alone, to be able to gaze on his face at leisure.

Bunthorne discovered him there and began to scowl threateningly.

"What is amiss?" asked Grosvenor.

Bunthorne accused him of monopolizing the attentions of the young ladies.

Those young ladies, responded Grosvenor, were the plague of his life. He wished someone would tell him how to escape from them.

Bunthorne offered to do so at once. He ordered Grosvenor to make a complete change in himself—keep his conversation commonplace, cut his hair, dress in ordinary clothing.

Grosvenor refused.

"Take care," Bunthorne warned him. "When I am thwarted I am very terrible."

"I can't help that," said Grosvenor. "I am a man with a mission, and that mission must be fulfilled."

"Suppose I were to curse you?" said Bunthorne.

Grosvenor began to tremble. "Say you will not do that!"

"Consent at once!" commanded Bunthorne, and Grosvenor yielded and went away.

"I have committed my last act of ill nature," said Bunthorne jubilantly, and he began to prance about, humming to himself.

Patience, coming through the woods, stopped to stare at his curious antics.

"I am a changed man," he told her. From this time on, he would be like Grosvenor—amusing and mildly cheerful.

"Oh, Reginald, I'm so happy!" she said. "It will no longer be a duty to love you, but a pleasure. Is it certain that you have reformed?"

It was *quite* certain, he assured her.

"Then I can no longer love you," she said, suddenly recollecting her duty. "Love must be unselfish. There can be nothing unselfish in loving so perfect a being as you have become."

Grosvenor came back to the glade, followed by the maidens, who were followed by the dragoons. Grosvenor was hardly recognizable. He had cut his hair and was wearing an ordinary suit of clothes. The maidens had cast aside their melancholy air and were dancing cheerfully and singing a song with Grosvenor.

"What does this mean?" asked Bunthorne.

It meant, said Angela, that Archibald the All-Right could not be all wrong. If he discarded his aesthetic ways, it was proof that they *ought* to be discarded.

Patience reproached Archibald. "I'm shocked—surprised —horrified!" she said.

He tried to explain that he was not to blame—that the change had been forced upon him.

"This is terrible!" she cried, and she ordered him out of her sight. Then a sudden thought came to her. "Is it quite, quite certain," she asked, "that you will *always* be a commonplace young man?"

"Always," he answered.

"Why, then," she said, "there is nothing to prevent my loving you."

"That's true," he agreed, and they embraced.

"Crushed again!" said Bunthorne.

"I am still here," said Lady Jane. "I have never left you, and I never will."

For the first time he began to look on her with favor. "Thank you, Jane," he said with real gratitude. "After all, there is no denying it, you're a fine figure of a woman."

The colonel, the major, and the duke joined the rest of the dragoons. The duke had made up his mind to choose a bride. He considered the maidens, while they fluttered excitedly.

He had great wealth to offer, he said. With their loveliness, the ladies already had all they needed to make them happy—except Jane, who was distinctly plain. Therefore he thought it only fair to choose her.

With no hesitation, Lady Jane left Bunthorne and threw herself into the duke's arms.

"Crushed again!" exclaimed Bunthorne.

Now that the duke and Jane were betrothed, the colonel chose Saphir, the major chose Angela, and Bunthorne's lawyer paired off with Ella.

There was no one left to be Bunthorne's bride, and while the others danced, he stood gazing at the lily he had taken from his buttonhole.

Iolanthe

or

THE PEER AND THE PERI

᠊ᴥᏜ *Gilbert based the story of* IOLANTHE *on one of his* BAB BALLADS. *The opera poked fun at British politics. It opened at the Savoy, D'Oyly Carte's new theater in London, on November 25, 1882, and was a tremendous success.*

A C T I ❧ Against a lovely Arcadian landscape, fairies—
or peris, as they were sometimes called—tripped hither and
thither. Leila, Celia, and Fleta led them in singing and
dancing, although none of them knew why they spent so
much time in motion. They were growing a little weary
of it all, and they sighed as they finished their song and dance.

They still missed their beloved sister, Iolanthe, who had
been banished from Fairyland. Fleta wondered what she
could have done to deserve so terrible a punishment.

"She married a mortal," Leila told her. "By our law, a
fairy who marries a mortal dies."

"But Iolanthe didn't die," said Celia.

The fairy queen explained why Iolanthe had been spared.
"Your queen, who loved her, commuted her sentence on
condition that she leave her husband and never communicate
with him again." Ever since, the banished fairy had lived at
the bottom of the stream nearby. She herself had chosen this
damp, unpleasant spot, and the queen had never understood
why.

"Why not ask her?" said Fleta.

"Because if I set eyes on her, I should forgive her," said
the queen.

"Then why not forgive her?" asked Celia. Iolanthe had
been in exile for twenty-five years. Surely this was punishment enough.

The queen let herself be persuaded. She and her fairies
called to Iolanthe.

The beautiful fairy rose from the stream. Humbly she knelt before the queen, who pardoned her. The fairies crowded about their sister, welcoming her back to the little band.

"Now tell me," said the queen, "with all the world to choose from, why did you decide to live at the bottom of that stream?"

"To be near my son, Strephon," answered Iolanthe.

The others were astonished. They had not known she had a son.

"He was born soon after I left my husband," she said. "He does not even know of his father's existence."

"How old is he?" asked Fleta.

"Twenty-four," replied Iolanthe.

"No one, to look at you, would think you had a son of twenty-four," marveled Leila. "But that's one advantage of being immortal. We never grow old."

Iolanthe told the fairies more about her son. He was a shepherd. He was in love with a girl named Phyllis. He was a handsome young man—a fairy down to his waist, with mortal legs.

The queen expressed a wish to see a person who was half fairy and half mortal.

"Nothing easier," said Iolanthe. "Here he comes."

Strephon came in sight. He greeted his mother with the news that he was to be married today.

"Then," she said, "the lord chancellor has at last given his consent to your marriage with his ward Phyllis?"

"Not he," said her son. The lord chancellor considered a mere shepherd unsuitable for his ward. Strephon and Phyllis were going to be married without her guardian's consent. "But what's this?" Strephon asked, seeing the other fairies for the first time.

"Rejoice with me," said his mother. "My queen has pardoned me."

"A pleasant piece of news for your bride on her wedding day," said the queen.

"Hush!" said Strephon. "My bride knows nothing of my fairyhood." He had not told her for fear of frightening her.

The queen was kindly disposed toward the young man. She promised to come to his aid in time of doubt or danger, and she and her band took gracious leave of him.

Phyllis joined Strephon, and they discussed the step they were about to take. It was a crime for her to marry without

the lord chancellor's consent. She suggested that they wait. In two years she would be of age. Then she could marry as she pleased.

Strephon was too much in love to consider waiting. Besides, he said, in two years she might fall in love with someone else—even the lord chancellor himself. As it was, half the peers in Parliament were sighing at her feet. "No," he said firmly, "delays are dangerous, and if we are to marry, the sooner the better."

He led her away.

A procession of peers came in sight, with the lord chancellor following. The peers were proud of their service to the government. Likewise, the lord chancellor took pride in

his office, although it had its disadvantages. As guardian of pretty young wards of the court, he spent his days giving agreeable girls away in marriage, without ever having one for himself.

Lord Tolloller arrived, ready to conduct the business of the day. The business had mainly to do with Phyllis. The peers were appealing to the lord chancellor to give her to one of them in marriage. Phyllis herself was to choose from among them.

It was a difficult decision for the lord chancellor, since he, too, loved Phyllis. But, he asked himself, could he give his own consent to his own marriage with his own ward? He was not certain. Therefore he bowed to the lords' wishes.

Lord Mountararat arrived to tell them that Phyllis had just consented to meet with the peers.

She came before them. They offered her their love and devotion, with all the wealth and position that accompanied their rank.

"You waste your time," she said. "My heart is given."

The peers were shocked.

"Who has dared to defy our command?" demanded the lord chancellor.

Strephon himself appeared to answer the question. "Against the world I claim my darling's hand!"

The peers bore up bravely under this blow and departed with the greatest dignity. The lord chancellor sent Phyllis away and challenged Strephon, "What excuse have you for having disobeyed an order of the court?"

Strephon replied that he knew no courts. He listened only to the commands of nature.

The lord chancellor refused to accept this as an excuse. He ridiculed the young man's reasoning and stalked away.

Iolanthe came upon the scene.

"Mother, weep with me!" cried Strephon, and he told her the tragic news—the lord chancellor had separated him from Phyllis forever.

Iolanthe was shaken at the mention of the lord chancellor, but she quickly recovered herself. "He has no power over you," she said. "Remember you are half a fairy. You can defy him—down to the waist."

"But from the waist downwards he can commit me to prison," said Strephon.

Iolanthe thought the matter should be placed before the fairy queen.

While she and her son were talking, the peers had been tiptoeing near, watching and listening. Lord Mountararat and Lord Tolloller led Phyllis between them.

Strephon said to his mother that when the day was dark, he would call on her to chase the gloom away.

"What was that?" whispered Phyllis.

Lord Mountararat whispered back that he thought he heard Strephon promise to call on her some rainy day.

Iolanthe said to her son that when all was drear and dark, if he should need an ark, she would get him one.

"What was that?" whispered Phyllis.

"I heard her say she'd meet him after dark in St. James's Park," Lord Tolloller whispered back.

Phyllis revealed herself and denounced Strephon. She had worshipped him blindly, she said, only to find that he worshipped someone else.

"The lady's my mother!" said Strephon.

The peers hooted in derision. The lord chancellor heard their laughter and returned. Iolanthe veiled her face as he came near.

He asked why the peers were laughing. Lord Mountararat replied that Strephon had tried to make them believe that this maiden, who looked no more than seventeen, was his mother.

Iolanthe *was* his mother, Strephon insisted hotly, but neither Phyllis nor the peers would believe him. In the confusion, Iolanthe slipped away.

"Go," Phyllis said to Strephon. "We must part forever." Now she was ready to give her hand to one of the lords. She narrowed her choice to Lord Mountararat and Lord Tolloller, but could not decide between them.

The fairy queen and her band came to Strephon's aid. "You've done him an injustice," said the queen to the lords. "The lady *is* his mother."

The lords mistook her for a teacher in a girls' school. They ordered her to take her brood and be off.

Turning on them in wrath, she identified herself as an influential fairy and vowed that when Parliament next assembled they would tremble. This was to be her revenge: She would seat Strephon in Parliament. If any bill or measure pleased him, it would be passed by both houses, no matter how much it angered the peers.

The lords were shaken. Phyllis implored Strephon's forgiveness. He thrust her away, and she fell fainting into the arms of Lord Mountararat and Lord Tolloller.

A C T I I ⅊ In the moonlit yard outside Westminster Palace, a lone guard was on sentry duty. The band of fairies appeared, chattering among themselves about Strephon's political career. Since he had been seated in Parliament, he had become a great power.

Lord Mountararat and Lord Tolloller came out of Westminster Hall, along with the other peers.

"You seem annoyed," Celia said to them.

"Annoyed! I should think so!" said Lord Mountararat. Strephon was making life very difficult for them. Any bill he favored was automatically passed.

The fairies were responsible for this, said Leila.

"Yes," said Celia, "we influence the members and compel them to vote just as he wishes them to."

Lord Mountararat said grimly, "This comes of women interfering in politics." He appealed to them to stop Strephon before it was too late.

"We can't stop him now," said Leila.

Once more she and her sisters declared themselves the enemies of the lords, and the men continued on their way. Yet it was plain that the fairies had not wanted them to go. When the queen appeared, she found her little band gazing longingly after the peers.

"Shame upon you," she reproved them. "Know you not that it is death to marry a mortal?"

"But it's not death to *wish* to marry a mortal," said Leila.

"This is weakness," the queen said sternly.

"We are not all as tough as you are," said Leila.

"Do you suppose *I* am insensible to the effect of manly beauty? Look at that man." The queen indicated the sentry in the yard. "A perfect picture. Who are you, sir?"

"Private Willis, B Company, First Grenadier Guards," replied the sentry.

"You're a very fine fellow, sir," said the queen.

"I am generally admired," said Willis.

The queen confessed to her fairies that the man had the

most extraordinary effect on her. If she allowed herself, she could fall down and worship him, but because she was strong she was able to cast the impulse from her. At all cost, they must maintain the fairy law!

The queen and her fairies tripped away.

Phyllis entered. She could not think why she was not in better spirits. She was engaged to two nobles at once, which should make any girl happy. Still she was miserable.

The two noblemen, Lord Mountararat and Lord Tolloller, had followed her. She asked if they had settled who was to be her husband.

"We would rather leave that to you," said Lord Tolloller.

Both were earls, both were rich, both were plain. Phyllis saw nothing to choose between them.

"The awkward part is," said Lord Tolloller to Lord Mountararat, "that if you rob me of the girl of my heart, we must fight and one of us must die. It's a family tradition. It's a painful position, for I have very strong regard for you, George."

Lord Mountararat was much affected. "My dear Thomas!" he said.

"You are very dear to me," said Lord Tolloller. "We were boys together."

But after a consultation in which Private Willis took part, the two peers concluded that, after all, love did rank above friendship.

Lord Mountararat and Lord Tolloller departed. Phyllis went away alone. Private Willis left his post.

The lord chancellor came into the courtyard, looking wretched and wan. He had not been able to rest because of his love for Phyllis. He thought of the nightmare he had

had, and after recalling it in every terrible detail, he fell exhausted upon a seat.

Lord Mountararat and Lord Tolloller found him there. He revealed to them the torture of his love for Phyllis. Not wishing to stand in the way of his happiness, they encouraged him to plead his cause. "Faint heart never won fair lady," they reminded him, and the three went away together, with the lord chancellor in a more cheerful frame of mind.

Strephon and his former sweetheart met in the courtyard.

"Phyllis!" he exclaimed. "But I suppose I should say 'my lady.' I have not yet been informed which title your ladyship has pleased to select."

"I haven't decided," she said aloofly. " *I* have no *mother* to advise *me*."

"I have," he said.

"Yes, a *young* mother," said Phyllis.

"Not young—a couple of centuries or so," said Strephon. "I've no longer any reason to conceal the fact. She's a fairy."

"A fairy!" said Phyllis. "Well—that would account for a good many things. Then I suppose *you* are a fairy."

He was, he answered, down to his waistcoat. He hadn't told her before because he was afraid it would cause her to dislike him.

"But I'd rather have half a mortal I do love than half a dozen I don't," she said. Now she understood his peculiar situation. After this, when she saw him kissing a very young lady, she would know it was only an elderly relative.

Strephon embraced her. They decided to marry without further delay.

Iolanthe appeared and kissed her future daughter-in-law.

Phyllis remembered her guardian, who still stood between

her and Strephon. Strephon asked his mother to go to the lord chancellor and plead for them.

"No, no. Impossible!" said Iolanthe.

"But our very lives depend on his consent," said Strephon.

"You can't refuse!" said Phyllis.

Iolanthe was agitated. "You know not what you ask. The lord chancellor is—my husband!" She said to Strephon, "My husband and your father!"

"Then our course is plain," said Phyllis. Once her guardian learned that Strephon was his son, there would be no further objection to the marriage.

"No, he must not know," said Iolanthe. "He believed me to have died childless. I am bound, under penalty of death, not to undeceive him. But see—he comes!"

Strephon and Phyllis hurried away. Iolanthe drew a veil over her face.

The lord chancellor was in high good humor. As a suitor, he had asked for Phyllis' hand. As her guardian, he had hesitated. Then, after a struggle with himself, he had given his consent. Now he considered himself engaged to his beautiful ward.

Iolanthe came toward him and begged him not to destroy Strephon's happiness. Her appeal touched him, but he stood firm in his decision to marry Phyllis.

"Behold—it may not be!" She lifted her veil.

"Iolanthe!" he exclaimed.

"I live," she said, "now let me die."

The queen had come with her band of fairies. She pronounced Iolanthe's fate: "Once again thy vows are broken. Death thy doom, and thou shalt die!"

She raised her spear.

"Hold!" cried Leila. "If Iolanthe must die, so must we all. As she has sinned, so have we."

She disclosed that she and all her sisters had secretly married peers.

The queen was nonplussed. Although she knew the erring fairies deserved death, she could hardly bring herself to destroy them all. "And yet the law is clear," she said, unfolding a manuscript and reading from it. "Every fairy must die who marries a mortal."

The lord chancellor's legal mind had been at work. "Allow me to make a suggestion," he said. "The thing is really quite simple—the insertion of a single word will do it. Let it stand that every fairy shall die who *doesn't* marry a mortal."

"Very well," said the queen, and she made the change on the manuscript. Private Willis and the peers had come in. She called Willis to her. "To save my life, it is necessary that I marry at once. How would you like to be a fairy guardsman?"

"Well, ma'am," he answered, "I don't think much of a British soldier who wouldn't ill-convenience himself to save a female in distress."

"You are a brave fellow." She caused wings to spring from his shoulders. "And you, my lords, will you join our ranks?"

Phyllis and Strephon entered in time to hear Lord Mountararat and Lord Tolloller speak for their colleagues. The peers were ready and willing to join the ranks.

"Then away we go," said the queen. Wings sprang from the shoulders of the lords, and they all made ready for their flight to Fairyland. There, they were sure, the men would be happy to exchange the House of Peers for the House of Peris.

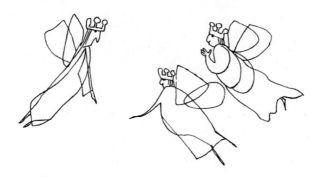

Princess Ida

or

CASTLE ADAMANT

◂§ *At the time* Gilbert *wrote the libretto of* PRINCESS IDA, *women were agitating for the right to vote. The opera satirized the "strong-minded" woman of the day. Gilbert's story was taken from his early play* THE PRINCESS, *which was in blank verse. He borrowed whole sections of the play for his libretto; thus* PRINCESS IDA *became Gilbert and Sullivan's only opera to be written in blank verse. It is also their only three-act opera.*

It was first produced at the Savoy Theatre in London on January 5, 1884.

ACT I 🐦 Soldiers and courtiers of King Hildebrand were outside the palace, anxiously scanning the landscape with telescopes. Royal visitors were expected—King Gama and his daughter, Ida.

King Hildebrand's son, Hilarion, had been betrothed to Ida when both were babies. On this day twenty years later King Gama had agreed to deliver his daughter to Prince Hilarion. If the royal party did not arrive by sunset, there would be war between the two nations.

The king came out into the pavilion with Cyril, a friend of his son's. They were joined by Florian, another of the prince's friends. King Hildebrand dreaded meeting King Gama, whom he described as a twisted monster with a disposition to match his body.

Looking through his glass, Florian spied King Gama's party on the distant mountain.

"Is the princess with him?" asked King Hildebrand.

Florian did not think she was, unless she was six feet tall, wore a mustache, and smoked cigars.

"One never knows," the king said moodily. He had heard she was a strange girl who did strange things.

He issued an order to his subjects. If King Gama had brought the princess, he was to receive a royal welcome. If not, he was to be thrown into the dungeon.

Prince Hilarion came out of the castle. He looked forward with joyful anticipation to Ida's coming, but he was fearful, too, thinking of the change that twenty years could bring.

The king broke the news to him that the royal party was arriving without the princess.

Prince Hilarion was not greatly surprised. He had heard that she had hidden herself away in a lonely palace, where she and a band of other women devoted themselves to higher learning. But this had not changed his feelings. She was his promised wife, and he had every intention of claiming her.

King Gama's sons—Arac, Guron and Scynthius—came to herald the arrival of the royal party. The three young men took pride in their skill as warriors, but admitted they were not intelligent.

King Gama entered. He was a misshapen little man, almost lost in his royal robes. He introduced himself as a genuine philanthropist, a person who recognized everyone else's faults and took pains to call attention to them. For this quality he was known as a disagreeable man. "And I can't think why," he said plaintively. He greeted King Hildebrand: "How old you've grown! Is this Hilarion? Why, you've changed, too. You were a handsome child."

King Hildebrand asked why Princess Ida had not come.

Because she had retired from the world to Castle Adamant, King Gama informed him. There she was head of a women's university with a hundred students.

"A hundred girls—a hundred ecstasies!" said Cyril, heaving a sigh.

The girls were not for him or for any other man, said King Gama. No males were allowed within the walls of Castle Adamant.

King Hildebrand determined to send Hilarion with an army to storm the castle. Meanwhile King Gama and his sons would remain as hostages. If harm should come to Hilarion, the hostages would be hanged.

Palace guards took King Gama and his sons into custody.

The prince planned his campaign. Cyril and Florian were to accompany him, and they would not use force. Expressive glances, flowers, and serenading would be the only weapons they would need.

ACT II ❧ Girl students were sitting at the feet of Lady Psyche, a professor, in the garden of Castle Adamant. Melissa, one of the girls, asked which classics she should read. Lady Psyche gave her a list and advised her to read the books from which all offending passages had been removed. Another girl, Sacharissa, asked for information on the thing known as man. Lady Psyche dismissed man as nature's mistake.

Lady Blanche, a professor who was also Melissa's mother, joined the group. She had brought Princess Ida's list of punishments, which she began to read. Sacharissa was to be expelled because she had brought a set of chessmen inside the walls. They were *men* and that was enough. Another girl, Chloe, was to be punished for having drawn a perambulator in her sketchbook.

Princess Ida came to give the usual address to the girls who had joined the group the day before. The students greeted her reverently as "mighty maiden with a mission."

She delivered her message. Woman was naturally superior to man; therefore woman had to conquer man and place her foot upon his neck.

She led the admiring students away, and Lady Blanche looked on enviously. "I should command here—I was born to rule," she told herself. Then she followed the others.

Prince Hilarion and his friends, Cyril and Florian, climbed over the wall and into the garden. They looked curiously about them. Some of the girls had left their academic robes behind. The men tried them on and minced about the garden, pretending they were lady students.

Princess Ida came upon them unexpectedly.

"What shall we do?" said Florian in a panic.

"We must brave it out," said Prince Hilarion. The men curtseyed to the princess and presented themselves as three well-born maids who wished to enter the university.

Princess Ida asked if they would abide by the rules and love their fellow students.

"Ma'am, we will!" promised Prince Hilarion with enthusiasm.

Also, said Princess Ida, they must swear that they would never marry any man.

Florian solemnly assured her, "Indeed, we never will."

"And have you left no lovers at home who may pursue you here?" asked Ida.

"No, madam," said Prince Hilarion. "We are homely ladies, as no doubt you see."

Their lack of beauty made no difference here, the princess assured them. "If all you say is true, you'll pass a happy time with us," she said, and she went away.

As the men burst out laughing, Lady Psyche came into the garden and surprised them.

Florian said to the prince, "Here's a catastrophe! This is my sister. She'll remember me."

There was nothing to do, said the prince, but to trust her with their secret.

"Psyche!" said Florian. "Don't you know me?"

"Why, Florian, what are you doing here?" she asked. "And who are these?"

The prince explained. Princess Ida was betrothed to him, and he had come to claim her.

Lady Psyche was alarmed. It was death for any man to be found here.

Melissa had come quietly up behind them. They discovered her listening to their conversation.

"All is lost!" said Lady Psyche.

But Melissa promised not to breathe a word. She was fascinated by the sight of Florian. "Is this a man?" she asked. "Till today I'd never set eyes on one. They told me men were hideous!" These she found even more beautiful than women.

Lady Psyche conducted the men out of the garden. Melissa had started after them, when her mother appeared and called her back.

"Those are the three new students?" asked Lady Blanche.

"Yes, they are," said Melissa. "They're charming girls."

"It's very odd," said Lady Blanche. "Two are tenors and one is a baritone."

"They've all got colds," said Melissa.

"Colds!" snorted Lady Blanche. "Do you think I am blind? These 'girls' are men disguised."

Melissa begged her mother to spare them. They were gentlemen, she said—Prince Hilarion and two trusted friends. The prince had come to claim the princess as his bride. She added cunningly, "Consider, you're only second here. Assist the prince's plan, and when he gains Princess Ida, you will be first."

The prospect tempted Lady Blanche. She let herself be persuaded.

She left the garden, and Florian came back, searching for Melissa. She urged him to leave. Her mother had guessed that he was a man and for reasons of her own had agreed to keep his secret, but still there was danger here. "Fly," she said, "and take me with you."

Before they could escape, the luncheon bell rang. The rest of the students descended upon them, along with Prince Hilarion, Princess Ida, Cyril, Lady Blanche, and Lady Psyche.

During the meal, Princess Ida spoke to the disguised prince. "You say you know the court of Hildebrand. There is a prince there—is he well?"

Prince Hilarion answered that he drooped and pined and sighed, "Oh, Ida, Ida!" all day long.

Cyril was tipsy from the wine he had been drinking. "Prince Hilarion's a goodly lad," he said heartily.

"You know him then?" asked Princess Ida.

"I rather think I do," said Cyril. "We are inseparables." He recalled a kissing song the prince had once sung, and he began to sing it.

Prince Hilarion and Florian tried to stop him. He shook them off and sang the song to the end.

The prince was furious. "Dog! This is something more to sing about!" he shouted, and he struck Cyril.

Cyril shouted back, "Hilarion, are you mad?"

"Help! These are *men!*" cried the princess. She fled to the bridge over the stream that ran through the garden. She lost her footing and fell into the water.

The prince plunged after her and carried her to safety.

But even though it was a man who had rescued her, the princess showed no mercy to the intruders. The female guards bound them and marched them off.

Melissa came forward with shocking news. King Hildebrand and an armed band were battering at the castle gate.

"We will defy them!" said the princess.

The gate burst open. King Hildebrand and his soldiers rushed in. King Gama's three sons were with them, still prisoners and still wearing handcuffs.

The king bluntly reminded Ida that she was promised to his son. If she broke the vow, he and his men would level the castle to the ground.

Not only that, added Ida's three brothers, but they were hostages and would be hanged if she continued to thwart the king.

"His threats are idle," said the princess. "He dares not kill you."

"We rather think he does," said the brothers gloomily, "but never mind."

King Hildebrand put an end to the parley. He gave the princess till the following afternoon to become Prince Hilarion's bride. If she did not comply, her brothers would be put to death.

Princess Ida hurled back defiance.

ACT III &sv The girl students were barricaded in the castle courtyard within the outer walls. They had armed themselves with battleaxes. Princess Ida entered, in battle array. Lady Blanche and Lady Psyche were her attendants.

The princess made a stirring speech. "We have to show that woman can meet man face to face on his own ground and beat him there." She asked, "Where is our surgeon?"

"Here," said Sacharissa. But although she had often healed the wounded in theory, she refused to consider doing it in practice.

"Coward!" said the princess. She asked why her soldiers were armed with battleaxes instead of rifles.

The rifles had been left in the armory, said Chloe, for fear they might go off.

"Where's my bandmistress?" asked the princess.

The members of the band did not feel well and could not come out today, reported another girl.

Princess Ida denounced them all and declared that she herself would care for the wounded, handle the firearms, and play trumpet music. She ordered them away and prepared to meet the men alone.

King Gama came tottering in. He was trembling and pale.

Princess Ida was astonished to see him there. "Father, you are free!"

He was not free, he answered. He had come with a message from King Hildebrand. When it was delivered, he must return to captivity. The message was this: King Hildebrand could not bring himself to make war against women. He was making a counterproposal—to pit King Gama's three sons against Prince Hilarion, Cyril, and Florian. The issue would be decided by the outcome of the battle.

Princess Ida was outraged. How did her father dare bring her such an insulting offer?

Her father answered brokenly that he was being tortured. King Hildebrand and his subjects were so polite, generous, and considerate that King Gama had nothing whatever to grumble at, and this—to him—was worse than death.

Princess Ida pitied him. She accepted King Hildebrand's terms.

The gates were opened. King Hildebrand's soldiers trooped in, bringing King Gama's three sons. Princess Ida's guards brought out Prince Hilarion, Cyril, and Florian.

King Gama and his sons taunted the three young men, who were still in women's clothing. The sons removed their armor before the fight, which they were sure would be an unequal one.

Prince Hilarion, Florian, and Cyril met the three warriors. The girl students looked down from the battlements, and although their duty to the princess was plain, they found themselves cheering for Prince Hilarion.

The fight was fierce. It ended with Gama's bewildered warriors on the ground, at the mercy of Prince Hilarion and his two friends.

Princess Ida moved to end the conflict. She asked Lady Blanche, "If I resign my post, will you take my place?"

Lady Blanche's answer showed her to be only too willing.

"I thought as much," said Princess Ida. So ended her cherished plan to band all women together against the tyranny of men. But, said she, if her scheme had succeeded, posterity would have honored her name.

If she had succeeded, returned King Hildebrand, there would *be* no posterity.

"Madam, you placed your trust in woman," said Prince Hilarion. "Woman has failed you. Try man."

"Remember too," said Cyril, "if at any time you feel weary of the prince, you can return to Castle Adamant."

"And shall I find the Lady Psyche here?" asked Princess Ida.

But Lady Psyche was already promised to Cyril, as Melissa was promised to Florian.

"Consider this, my love," King Gama pointed out to his daughter, "if your mamma had looked on matters from your point of view, where would you be?"

"I have been wrong—I see my error now," said Princess Ida, and she gave Prince Hilarion her hand.

The Mikado

or

THE TOWN OF TITIPU

~§ *During the run of* PRINCESS IDA, *Gilbert was considering what he and Sullivan would write next. Interest in Japan was high in England. Japanese art was popular. Visitors were flocking to a Japanese exhibit that had opened in London. Gilbert hit on the idea of a Japanese opera and spent six months writing the libretto of* THE MIKADO.

He hired a geisha girl from the exhibit and brought her to rehearsals. Her English was limited to "sixpence, please" —sixpence being the price of a cup of tea at the exhibit— but she taught the cast authentic Japanese mannerisms.

From its first performance, at the Savoy Theatre on March 14, 1885, THE MIKADO *has remained the most popular Gilbert and Sullivan opera. The story is more than a ludicrous picture of Japanese life. It is a satire on political corruption in any government.*

111

ACT I 𝔢 Outside the lord high executioner's palace in the Japanese town of Titipu, noblemen were standing or sitting in picturesque attitudes, when a young man named Nanki-Poo dashed into the courtyard. A native guitar was slung on his back; a sheaf of ballads was in his hand. Anxiously he inquired where he might find the gentle maiden named Yum-Yum.

"Who are you to ask this question?" they asked.

He replied that he was a wandering minstrel, who sang songs for all occasions.

Pish-Tush, a noble lord, wanted to know what his business might be with Yum-Yum.

Nanki-Poo told his story. A year ago, when he was playing second trombone in the Titipu band, he and Yum-Yum had met and fallen in love. But she was betrothed to her guardian, a tailor named Ko-Ko. In despair Nanki-Poo left town and traveled far away. Then, a month ago, the news reached him that Ko-Ko had been condemned to death for flirting. Nanki-Poo had hurried back, hoping to find Yum-Yum free.

The news was true, said Pish-Tush. Ko-Ko *had* been condemned to death, but at the last moment he had been reprieved and raised to the rank of lord high executioner under these remarkable circumstances:

The Mikado, ruler of Japan, wished Japanese men to be serious-minded, and he had decreed that all who flirted or winked or leered should be beheaded. This was a most unpopular law. The people of Titipu had sought to circumvent it, so the man whose head was next to be cut off had been released from the Titipu jail and given the post of lord high executioner. It was ruled that the executioner could not cut off anyone else's head until he had first cut off his own. This ruling put an end to all executions and made the public happy. And Ko-Ko was happy at having been elevated to the rank of lord high executioner.

Pooh-Bah, a haughty nobleman, volunteered more information. All the important government officials in Titipu had resigned rather than serve under an ex-tailor. Pooh-Bah had accepted their positions. He was now all the officials rolled into one. Knowing himself to be proud, he was continually trying to overcome this defect in his character. Therefore he humiliated himself by taking pay for his services.

"I also retail state secrets at a very low figure," he said. "For instance, any further information about Yum-Yum would come under the head of a state secret."

Nanki-Poo took the hint and crossed Pooh-Bah's hand with money.

Pooh-Bah went on to say that today the fair Yum-Yum would return home from school to marry Ko-Ko.

Nanki-Poo went sadly away.

Ko-Ko entered with a train of attendants. The noblemen bowed low before him.

He thanked them and expressed the hope that he would always deserve their favors. He promised that if he should ever be called on to perform his public duties, he could easily find plenty of people whose execution would be a benefit to society. He had a little list, he said—a list of those who never would be missed.

A group of schoolgirls entered the courtyard, followed
by three little maids—Yum-Yum, Peep-Bo, and Pitti-Sing—
who had just finished their education at a ladies' seminary.

Ko-Ko embraced his bride-to-be. She dutifully accepted
his attentions; then she and her two friends ran to talk with
Nanki-Poo, who had just returned.

"I beg your pardon," said Ko-Ko. "Will you present me?"
Yum-Yum introduced the two men.

"Sir, I have the misfortune to be in love with your ward,"
said Nanki-Poo. "I know I deserve your anger."

"Anger? Not a bit, my boy. Why, I love her myself," said

Ko-Ko blandly. But for all his apparent generosity, he had Pish-Tush remove Nanki-Poo.

Ko-Ko introduced Pooh-Bah to the girls. They laughed at the nobleman's pompous airs.

"Don't mind them," said Ko-Ko. "They don't understand the delicacy of your position."

He left Pooh-Bah with the girls. They apologized for their behavior. He reproved them—not too severely—and went away. All the others left except Yum-Yum.

Nanki-Poo found her there. "At last we are alone," he said. "I had sought you night and day in the belief that your guardian was beheaded, and I find you are to be married to him this afternoon."

"Alas, yes," said Yum-Yum.

"Why do you not refuse him?" asked Nanki-Poo.

"What good would that do?" said Yum-Yum. "He's my guardian, and he wouldn't let me marry you." Besides, she told him, a wandering minstrel was hardly a proper husband for the ward of the lord high executioner.

"Shall I tell her?" said Nanki-Poo to himself. "Yes!" He asked Yum-Yum, "What if it should prove that I am no musician? What if it should prove that I am no other than the son of His Majesty the Mikado?"

"The son of the Mikado!" said Yum-Yum in amazement. "But why is Your Highness disguised? What has Your Highness done?"

Some years ago, he told her, an elderly lady of his father's court, named Katisha, had fallen in love with him. The Mikado ordered him to marry her within a week or perish on the scaffold. Nanki-Poo fled the court and had since been traveling the country in the guise of a wandering musician.

He came close to Yum-Yum. She drew away, reminding him of the laws against flirting.

If it were not for the law, he sighed, how happy they might be! They talked of how they might embrace and kiss, if she were not promised to Ko-Ko.

"But *this*," he said, kissing her, "is what I'll never do." And they went away in opposite directions.

Ko-Ko entered and looked tenderly after Yum-Yum. Pish-Tush and Pooh-Bah came into the courtyard. Pish-Tush had a letter for Ko-Ko—a letter from the Mikado.

Ko-Ko read the message. The news was disastrous. The Mikado noted that no executions had taken place in Titipu for a year. He decreed that unless somebody was beheaded within one month, the post of lord high executioner would be abolished and the town of Titipu reduced to the rank of a village.

They would all be ruined, moaned Pish-Tush.

"I shall have to execute somebody," said Ko-Ko. "The only question is, who shall it be?"

"As you're already under sentence of death for flirting," said Pooh-Bah, "everything seems to point to *you*."

Ko-Ko considered the suggestion impractical. "I can't execute myself."

"Why not?" asked Pooh-Bah.

There were two reasons, said Ko-Ko. First, it was extremely difficult to cut off one's own head. Second, suicide was a crime, punishable by death.

Still Pooh-Bah and Pish-Tush thought Ko-Ko should at least *try* to cut off his head, as evidence of good faith. Pish-Tush could see no other way, unless a substitute could be found.

Ko-Ko seized on the idea. "A substitute? Oh, certainly," and he appointed Pooh-Bah lord high substitute.

Pooh-Bah declined the honor. It was really his fondest dream, he said, but he must set a limit on his ambitions.

He and Pish-Tush went away, leaving Ko-Ko to reflect on Pooh-Bah's ingratitude. Nanki-Poo crossed the courtyard, carrying a rope.

"What are you going to do?" asked Ko-Ko.

Nanki-Poo answered that he was about to end his life.

"Nonsense! What for?" asked Ko-Ko.

"Because you are going to marry the girl I adore," said Nanki-Poo.

At first Ko-Ko declared that he would not permit such a cold-blooded crime. Then an idea struck him. "Substitute!" he told himself, and he said to Nanki-Poo, "If you are absolutely resolved to die, don't spoil yourself by committing suicide. Have yourself beheaded handsomely at the hands of the executioner." This would give the young man a month to live. He would be the central figure in the execution. Bands would play; there would be a parade; Yum-Yum would be distracted—

Nanki-Poo had an idea of his own. "Let me marry Yum-Yum tomorrow, and in a month you may behead me."

"No, no," said Ko-Ko. "I draw the line at Yum-Yum."

"If you draw the line, so do I," said Nanki-Poo, and he began to prepare the rope.

Ko-Ko stopped him. "Be reasonable. How can I consent to your marrying Yum-Yum if I'm going to marry her myself?"

"My good friend, she'll be a widow in a month," said Nanki-Poo, "and you may marry her then."

With great reluctance, Ko-Ko agreed to the plan.

Pooh-Bah and Pish-Tush returned with the other gentlemen. "Congratulate me. I've found a volunteer," said Ko-Ko. "He yields his life if I'll surrender Yum-Yum."

Yum-Yum came in with Peep-Bo and Pitti-Sing.

"Take her—she's yours," Ko-Ko said to Nanki-Poo with a grand gesture, and he hurried off.

Everyone present knew that Nanki-Poo and Yum-Yum would have only a month together; yet, as Pitti-Sing said, "You'll live at least a honeymoon."

There were joyous festivities. At the height of the merriment a fierce-eyed, elderly lady swept into the courtyard.

"Your revels cease!" she cried.

In a panic, Nanki-Poo whispered to Yum-Yum that the woman was Katisha, who had caused him to flee from his father's court. He tried to escape, but Katisha detained him. "You shall not go. These arms shall thus enfold you!"

She denounced him for leaving the joys of her love, and she prophesied the doom of Yum-Yum.

Pitti-Sing defied the raging woman. "Away! From our intention you cannot turn us, for he's going to marry Yum-Yum!"

Katisha swore that the faithless Nanki-Poo would regret this insult. "Prepare yourselves for news surprising," she said. "He is the son of your—"

Before she could speak the final word, Nanki-Poo and Yum-Yum interrupted, drowning out her voice. Again and again she tried to speak. Each time all the others kept her from being heard. At last, in helpless fury, she thrust her way through the crowd and disappeared.

ACT II ❧ Yum-Yum was seated in Ko-Ko's garden. Maidens were dressing her hair and painting her face for the wedding. The bride was beautiful. She was to be married to the man she loved. Still it was hard to pretend that the occasion was a happy one. The maidens kept reminding her that in a month her bliss would be cut short.

Nanki-Poo arrived with words of cheer. Pish-Tush joined them. Pish-Tush, Pitti-Sing, and the bridal pair sang a gay madrigal, but the song ended in tears.

Ko-Ko entered. "My child—my poor child!" he greeted Yum-Yum. "My little bride that was to have been."

"*Was* to have been?" said Yum-Yum.

"Yes," said Ko-Ko dolefully. "You can never be mine." According to the Mikado's law, he informed them, when a man was beheaded his wife was buried alive.

Yum-Yum looked at Nanki-Poo. "It—it does make a difference, doesn't it?" she said.

He agreed that it did. "If I insist on your carrying out your promise, I doom you to death. If I release you, you marry Ko-Ko."

It was a pretty state of things, they all told one another. Weeping, Yum-Yum went away. "But you shan't be disappointed of a wedding," Ko-Ko said to Nanki-Poo. "You shall come to mine."

That would be impossible, said Nanki-Poo. He could not live without Yum-Yum. Today he was committing suicide.

"Hang it all, you're under contract to die by the hand of the executioner in a month's time!" said Ko-Ko in exasperation. "If you kill yourself, what's to become of me? I shall have to be executed in your place."

Pooh-Bah came to announce that the Mikado and his party were just outside the town.

"The Mikado!" exclaimed Ko-Ko, shuddering. "He's coming to see whether his orders have been carried out. Now look here," he said to Nanki-Poo, "a bargain's a bargain, and you really mustn't frustrate justice by committing suicide."

"Very well, then," said Nanki-Poo. "Behead me."

But this was no more to Ko-Ko's liking. He was a tender-hearted man, an executioner in title only. "I *can't* kill you— I can't kill anybody!" he sobbed.

"If I don't mind, why should you?" said Nanki-Poo. "Remember, sooner or later it must be done."

Perhaps there was another way, said Ko-Ko. Perhaps they could *pretend* that Nanki-Poo had been executed. He listed the high government officials who would swear they had witnessed the act.

"But where are they?" asked Nanki-Poo.

Ko-Ko pointed to Pooh-Bah. Pooh-Bah was all these officials in one, and for a cash bribe he would sign any affidavit.

"But I tell you life without Yum-Yum—" began Nanki-Poo.

"Oh, bother Yum-Yum!" broke in Ko-Ko. "Take Yum-Yum and marry Yum-Yum, only go away and never come back!"

Pooh-Bah brought in Yum-Yum.

"Go along with the Archbishop of Titipu," said Ko-Ko.

"He'll marry you at once. Don't ask any questions. Do as I tell you."

And Yum-Yum and Nanki-Poo went along with Pooh-Bah, who was the Archbishop of Titipu.

Ko-Ko breathed a sigh of relief. His main concern had been to get Nanki-Poo out of sight before the Mikado arrived. Now he prepared to save his own life by pretending he had executed the young man.

He left the garden as the Mikado and Katisha entered, accompanied by their attendants.

The Mikado made a speech in which he discussed crime and punishment. The object of his rule, he said, was to let the punishment fit the crime.

Ko-Ko brought in Pooh-Bah and Pitti-Sing.

"Your Majesty's wish has been attended to. The execution has taken place," said Ko-Ko, and he handed a paper to the Mikado.

The paper was the death certificate signed by the coroner. Pooh-Bah was the coroner.

Ko-Ko, Pitti-Sing, and Pooh-Bah described the imaginary execution in vivid detail.

"This is very interesting," said the Mikado, "but we came about a different matter. A year ago my son bolted from our Imperial Court and is now masquerading in this town. He goes by the name of Nanki-Poo."

Katisha had been reading the death certificate. "See here —his name—Nanki-Poo—beheaded this morning." She began to wail. "Oh, where shall I find another!"

Ko-Ko, Pooh-Bah, and Pitti-Sing looked at one another in consternation. They fell to their knees.

The Mikado said to Ko-Ko, "My poor fellow, you have beheaded the heir to the throne of Japan."

Ko-Ko, Pooh-Bah, and Pitti-Sing offered abject apologies.

"We really hadn't the least notion—" said Pitti-Sing.

"Of course you hadn't," said the Mikado kindly. "How could you?"

They rose, thanking him for his generosity.

The Mikado casually mentioned the punishment for bringing about the death of the heir to the throne. He fancied it had something to do with boiling oil or melted lead. "Come, come, don't fret," he said to Ko-Ko, Pooh-Bah, and Pitti-Sing, who had fallen to their knees again in terror. "I'm not a bit angry." Unfortunately there was no provision in the law for "not knowing" or "having no notion." It was foolish, but it was the law. "Now, let's see about your executions," he said. "Can you wait till after luncheon?"

"Oh, yes—we can wait," said Ko-Ko, Pitti-Sing, and Pooh-Bah.

"I'm really very sorry for you," said the Mikado, "but it's an unjust world."

He and Katisha went away.

Ko-Ko, Pooh-Bah, and Pitti-Sing turned on one another. Each blamed the other for their predicament. There was only one thing to do, said Ko-Ko. They must bring Nanki-Poo back to life.

Nanki-Poo and Yum-Yum came through the garden, dressed for a journey.

"Here, I've good news for you," said Ko-Ko. "You've been reprieved."

"It's too late," said Nanki-Poo. "I'm a dead man, and I'm off for my honeymoon."

"Nonsense! It seems you're the son of the Mikado," said Ko-Ko. "Your father is here—with Katisha. He wants you particularly."

"So does she," said Pooh-Bah.

"But Nanki-Poo is married now," said Yum-Yum.

"What has that to do with it?" Ko-Ko wanted to know.

Nanki-Poo summed up the state of affairs. "Katisha claims me in marriage, but I can't marry her because I'm married already. Consequently she will insist on my execution. And if I'm executed, my wife will have to be buried alive."

Ko-Ko said wretchedly, "I don't know what's to be done."

Nanki-Poo had a suggestion. "If you can persuade Katisha to marry *you*, she will have no further claim on me. Then I can come to life without any fear of being put to death."

"I marry Katisha?" Ko-Ko was horrified. "Have you seen her? She's something appalling!"

"It comes to this," said Nanki-Poo. "When Katisha is single, I prefer to be a spirit. When Katisha is married, existence will be as welcome as the flowers in spring."

The prospect was a hideous one for Ko-Ko, but he had no choice. Trying to make the best of the situation, he left with the others.

Katisha appeared, tragic in her bereavement. Ko-Ko had followed her. Timidly he begged for mercy.

"See here, you!" said Katisha. "You have slain my love. He did not love *me*, but he *would* have loved me in time. Well, he is dead, and where shall I find another? It takes years to train a man to love me. Oh, where shall I find another?"

"Here," said Ko-Ko.

"What?" cried Katisha.

With intense passion he declared his affection for her. "Accept my love, or I perish on the spot."

She scornfully observed that no one had ever yet died of a broken heart.

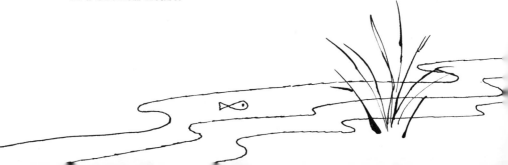

"You know not what you say. Listen," Ko-Ko said, and he told her a pathetic tale of a bird that had committed suicide because of a hopeless love.

The story reduced Katisha to tears. She began to whimper over the fate of the poor little bird. "And if I refuse you, will you do the same thing?" she asked.

"At once," he assured her.

"No—no, you mustn't," said Katisha, and she threw herself into his arms.

They quickly discovered that all in all their tastes were quite similar, and they left the garden together, planning to marry without delay.

The Mikado came back with his courtiers and Pish-Tush in attendance. They had had a good lunch. Now they were ready for the executions.

Ko-Ko, Pooh-Bah, and Pitti-Sing were brought in. Katisha was with them, and they all threw themselves at the Mikado's feet.

"Mercy for Ko-Ko! Mercy for Pitti-Sing!" pleaded Katisha. "Mercy even for Pooh-Bah!"

She had just married Ko-Ko, she said. The registrar had performed the ceremony. Pooh-Bah was the registrar.

The Mikado was sympathetic, but legally he could show no mercy, since the prisoners had slain the heir to the throne.

Nanki-Poo and Yum-Yum came forward and knelt at his feet. "The heir is *not* slain," said Nanki-Poo.

"Bless my heart, my son!" said the Mikado.

"And your daughter-in-law," said Yum-Yum.

Ko-Ko, with help from Pooh-Bah, explained all that had happened and the Mikado found the explanation perfectly satisfactory. Nanki-Poo and Yum-Yum told each other, "The threatened cloud has passed away, and brightly shines the dawning day."

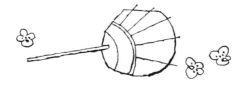

Ruddigore

or

THE WITCH'S CURSE

~§ *The run of* THE MIKADO *was so long and so successful that it was two years before the partners gave much thought to their next work. Gilbert suggested an old-fashioned melodrama with curses, ghosts, and theatrical villains. Sullivan was pleased with the idea, and Gilbert brought him the story of* RUDDIGORE. *The opera was first performed at the Savoy Theatre on January 22, 1887.*

129

ACT I ❧ A group of professional bridesmaids ranged themselves outside Rose Maybud's cottage in the Cornish village of
Rederring. They were required to be on duty every day from
ten to four, but for months no one had needed their services.
Since they were eager to practice their profession and since
Rose was the loveliest maiden in the village, they had come
to her door to ask, "Is anybody going to marry you today?"

Rose's aunt, Dame Hannah, stepped out of the cottage to
tell the girls that Rose's heart was still free.

It was very disappointing, complained Zorah, one of the
bridesmaids. Every young man in the village was in love with
Rose, but her beauty and modesty kept them at a distance.
Until she made her choice, there was no chance for any other
young woman, so there were no marriages in Rederring.

"Dame Hannah, *you* could marry if you liked," said
Zorah.

Dame Hannah replied that she would never wed. Many
years ago she had been disappointed in love. She was betrothed to a man who courted her under an assumed name.
Just before the marriage was to have taken place, she discovered him to be Sir Roderic Murgatroyd, one of the bad
baronets of Ruddigore. He was no husband for a respectable
girl, so she left him.

"Why shouldn't you marry a bad baronet of Ruddigore?"
asked Zorah.

"Was he worse than other baronets?" asked Ruth, another bridesmaid.

"My child, he was accursed," said Hannah, and she told the legend of the Murgatroyds. Sir Rupert, first of his line, had made a sport of persecuting witches. Once when he was having one burned at the stake, she placed this curse on him: "Each lord of Ruddigore shall commit one crime each day or die in torture." Ever afterward each heir who held the title had been forced to commit a crime each day, until bowed down with guilt, he had vowed to sin no more. And on that day he had died in agony.

When they heard this, the horrified bridesmaids departed.

Rose Maybud came out of her cottage with a basket on her arm. She was taking gifts to deserving villagers.

It was a pity, said Hannah, that so much goodness could not make some young man happy. She asked her niece, "Is there no one here whom you could love?"

If there were, said Rose, it would not be proper for her to tell him so. This she had learned from a book of etiquette, which had been her guide in life and which she carried with her constantly.

Dame Hannah spoke of young Robin Oakapple, whose manners and morals were certainly above reproach. "Could you not love him?" she asked.

Rose answered that even if she could, she had no way of letting him know, and he was too shy to speak.

Dame Hannah went her way. Rose was about to leave, when Robin came up to the cottage. Because of his shyness, he could not speak what was in his heart. Maidenly modesty kept her from revealing her feelings. Instead, each asked the other's advice about a "friend."

His friend loved a maid but was too timid to tell her so. Her friend was sick with love for a young man but could not bring herself to let him know.

"If I were the maid, I should meet the lad halfway," said Robin.

"If I were the youth, I should speak to her today," said Rose.

He thanked her for her advice, she thanked him for his, and there seemed no more to say. She left on her charitable errands.

Old Adam Goodheart, Robin's faithful servant, came upon the scene. "My master is sad," he said. "Dear Sir Ruthven Murgatroyd—"

Robin silenced him. "Breathe not that hated name!" Twenty years ago he had fled his home to avoid inheriting the hideous title that would have forced him to commit a crime a day. He had changed his name and lived as a farmer. His younger brother, Despard, believing him dead, had taken over the title and the curse. "For twenty years I have been dead and buried," Robin told his servant. "Don't dig me up now."

"Dear master, it shall be as you wish," said Old Adam. "But I bring you good tidings. Your foster-brother, Richard, has returned from sea and is on his way here."

The bridesmaids were on hand to welcome Richard when he came into the village. He told them a tale of life at sea. Then after they had gone, he greeted Robin, whom he had not seen for ten years.

He noticed that Robin looked sad, and he asked the reason.

"Ah, Dick," said Robin, "I love Rose Maybud, and love in vain."

This was hard for Richard to grasp. Was not Robin a fine young fellow and a nobleman, to boot?

"Not a word about my true rank," Robin cautioned him. "Yes, I know well enough I'm a fine fellow—happy the girl who gets me. But I'm timid, Dick. I cannot tell her."

"Do you call to mind how years ago we swore we would always act upon our hearts' dictates?" asked Richard. "Well now, what does my heart say in this difficult situation? It says, 'Dick, *you* ain't shy—speak up for him!'"

Robin was delighted with the idea, and he left his foster-brother to carry it out.

Rose came in sight. Richard was dazzled by her charms.

"Sir, you are agitated," she said.

"Aye, I am agitated, true enough," he said. He had meant to speak for his foster-brother, but his heart said, "Dick this is the very lass for *you*," and he began speaking eloquently for himself.

Rose consulted her etiquette book. "Keep no one in unnecessary suspense," she read, so she accepted him at once.

Robin came back with the bridesmaids.

"What news?" he asked. "Have you spoken to her?"

Richard confessed that his heart had spoken instead. "It's like this," he said. "She accepted—but it's *me*."

The bridesmaids began to sing, "Hail the bridegroom—hail the bride!"

"Hold your tongues!" said Robin angrily, and he drove them off. He tried to be reasonable, but he could not help showing his disappointment.

Now that Rose knew his true feelings, she declared that it was really Robin she loved. The three went away, with Richard weeping.

A strange figure in rags and tatters came running through the village. She sang and laughed wildly. "Who am I?" she cried. "Crazy Meg! Mad Margaret!"

Rose approached and sympathetically offered the girl an apple.

Mad Margaret refused it. "Tell me, are you mad?" she asked.

"I think not," said Rose.

"Then you don't love Sir Despard Murgatroyd," said Margaret. "All mad girls love him. *I* love him." She whispered, "I have come to pinch Rose Maybud." She feared that Sir Despard might see the lovely Rose and try to make her his.

"Behold, I am Rose Maybud," said Rose. "I am pledged to another, and we are to be wedded this very day."

135

"Swear me that!" said Margaret eagerly. "But see, they come—Sir Despard and his evil crew. Hide, hide!" And she tiptoed away, drawing Rose after her.

A group of gentlemen came into the village. The adoring bridesmaids accompanied them. Last came Sir Despard. He was a moody, guilt-ridden man, tortured by the Murgatroyd curse.

All the others fled from him as he prepared to commit his daily crime.

They loathed him, he thought; little did they know how pure he was at heart. In his castle there was a whole picture gallery of ancestors who stepped down from their frames and threatened him if he refused to commit a crime each day. But he managed to even the score. He got his crime over the first thing in the morning and spent the rest of the day doing good.

Richard came upon him. In a roundabout way he brought up the subject of Sir Despard's brother.

His brother was dead, said Sir Despard.

It was not so, Richard informed him. "He lives in this village under the name of Robin Oakapple, and he's going to marry Rose Maybud this very day."

Sir Despard was elated. He could shift the burden of the curse to his brother's shoulders. At last he could be free to lead a blameless life!

He and Richard left together. The bridesmaids and the young gentlemen congregated. The bride and groom arrived, ready for the marriage ceremony. Rose was attended by Zorah and Dame Hannah. Robin's attendants were Old Adam and Richard, who had doubled back and joined the group.

The wedding party celebrated with singing and dancing.

At the end of the dance, Sir Despard stepped forward and said for all to hear, "I claim Robin as my older brother!"

"Deny this falsehood!" cried Rose, and Robin answered miserably, "I would if I could, but I cannot."

She bade him farewell and said to Sir Despard, "Take me—I am your bride."

"Hail the bridegroom—hail the bride!" sang the bridesmaids.

Mad Margaret had come near and stood listening.

"Excuse me," Sir Despard said to Rose. "I'm a virtuous person now, and I must keep my vow to Margaret."

Margaret was overjoyed.

"I once disliked you," Sir Despard told her. "Now that I've reformed, how I adore you!"

"Hail the bridegroom—hail the bride!" sang the bridesmaids.

Rose turned to Richard. "You are the only one that's left," she said, "so I am yours."

Again the bridesmaids began their song. Robin alone was unhappy. Not only was he bereft of Rose, but he had become the latest victim of the Murgatroyd curse.

ACT II ❧ It was a week since the brothers had exchanged places. Robin and Old Adam were in the picture gallery of Ruddigore Castle. Already they were greatly altered. Robin looked haggard and oppressed by sin, and a wicked leer had replaced Old Adam's kindly expression.

"What crime do you propose to commit today?" asked the servant.

"How should I know?" said Robin. "As my confidential adviser, it's your duty to suggest something."

"Richard is here with pretty Rose Maybud to ask your consent to their marriage," said Old Adam. "Poison their beer."

Robin refused. "I know I'm bad, but not as bad as all that."

He and Old Adam stepped outside, as the bridesmaids conducted Richard and Rose into the gallery.

Robin came back to confront Rose. "In my power at last!" he said fiendishly, and threatened to call on forces of darkness that would carry her off to a dungeon.

But Richard was prepared for this. He whipped out a Union Jack. "Here is a flag that none dare defy," he said, "and while it floats over Rose Maybud's head, the man does not live who would dare lay a hand upon her."

"Foiled," muttered Robin, "and by a Union Jack!"

Rose tried to reason with him. There was nothing in the etiquette book that covered her case, but she hoped he would

138

be unselfish enough to consent to her marriage with Richard.

"Take her—I yield," said Robin to his foster-brother, and the visitors trooped away.

Robin looked up at the full-length ancestral portraits on the wall. The first was Sir Rupert, earliest victim of the curse. The last was of Sir Roderic, who had been deceased only for the past ten years.

Robin spoke to the pictures and asked them to soften their hearts toward him.

The lights dimmed. The portraits began to move. Slowly they stepped out of their frames and began to march about. The specter of Sir Roderic was the last to come down from his frame.

"Alas, poor ghost!" said Robin.

But Sir Roderic wanted no sympathy. "We specters are a jollier crew than you suppose," he said, and he described some of their midnight revels.

Robin asked why the pictures had left their frames.

It was their duty, said Sir Roderic, to see that their successors committed the required crimes in a workmanlike fashion. He asked Robin what evil things he had done during his first week as a bad baronet.

Robin listed his crimes. To the jury of ghosts, they were not impressive. Sir Roderic thought something serious should be added to the list—like carrying off a lady.

"Certainly not," said Robin. "I've the greatest respect for ladies."

The ghosts began to make gestures, and Robin writhed in agony.

"Don't do that!" he moaned. "I can't stand it!" And he promised that their will should be done.

The ghosts stepped back into their frames and became pictures again.

Old Adam looked in. Robin was pale and shaken. "I must do something desperate at once or perish!" he cried. "Go to yonder village—carry off a maiden—bring her here—anyone —I don't care which!"

Old Adam rushed off. Robin said farewell to the last remnants of his virtue, and he, too, rushed out of the detested picture gallery.

Despard and Margaret entered. They had been married a week. Both were dressed in sober black. Both conducted themselves with an air of the utmost respectability. But traces of Margaret's wildness remained, and from time to time her husband had to restrain her. They were now District Visitors. It was their duty to visit the sick, the poor, and the evil-doers.

Robin received them. They had come, Despard said, to beg him to give up his wicked ways. So persuasive were they that Robin promised to defy his ancestors and refuse to obey their commands, even though his defiance might well end in death.

Despard and Margaret left him.

Old Adam found Robin in the gallery. "Master, the deed is done," he said. "She is here."

Robin had forgotten his orders to the servant. "Who?" he asked.

"The maiden," said Old Adam. "I had a hard task, for she fought like a tiger-cat."

He pushed the captive into the room.

Robin gasped. The maiden was Dame Hannah!

She produced a dagger and threatened him.

"Don't! I can't stand it!" he called out. "Roderic! Uncle! Save me!"

The specter of Sir Roderic stepped down from his picture. "What's the matter?" he asked.

Hannah stared at him. Sir Roderic stared back. "My old love!" He turned accusingly to Robin. "What do you mean

by carrying off this lady? Are you aware that once she was engaged to be married to me? I'm very angry indeed."

He sent Robin away. He said to Hannah, "This is a strange meeting after so many years."

"Very," she agreed. "I thought you were dead."

"I am," he said. "I died ten years ago."

"And are you pretty comfortable?" she asked.

He replied that he was.

"You don't deserve to be," she reproached him. "I loved you, and it made me dreadfully unhappy to hear of all your goings-on." She compared herself to a little flower and Sir

Roderic to a great oak tree. Even though the oak had been unfaithful, the little flower remained true to his memory.

Robin came back into the gallery. The bridesmaids and the gentlemen were with him, and Richard, Rose, Despard, and Margaret.

Roderic and Hannah were annoyed by the interruption.

"I can't stop to apologize," Robin said excitedly. "An idea has just occurred to me. A baronet of Ruddigore can die only through refusing to commit his daily crime."

This was true, said Sir Roderic.

Then, said Robin, refusing to commit a daily crime was the same as suicide.

Sir Roderic agreed.

"But suicide is in itself a crime," said Robin, "and so you ought never to have died at all!"

"I see—I understand!" exclaimed Sir Roderic. "Then I'm practically alive!" and he embraced Dame Hannah.

Robin reminded Rose that she had loved him when he was a simple farmer. Then, when he became a bad baronet, she had very properly loved Richard instead. "But if I turn out *not* to be a bad baronet after all, how would you love me?" he asked.

"Madly, passionately!" said Rose.

"My darling!" said Robin.

After a moment of disappointment, Richard transferred his affections to Zorah, and happiness reigned at last in the gloomy halls of Ruddigore Castle.

The Yeomen of
the Guard

or

THE MERRYMAN AND HIS MAID

The Yeomen of the Guard is the oldest English military corps. It was established in 1485 as the personal guard of the ruling monarch. Later the yeomen, or beefeaters, served as guards to the Tower of London. Over the centuries their uniform has remained the same—black hat; white ruff; tunic of red, purple, and gold; red knee breeches and hose; and shoes with black rosettes.

One day Gilbert saw a poster of a beefeater in his colorful costume. The picture suggested to him the plot of an opera about the Tower of London. He wrote the libretto, taking great pains with it, and was happy with the result. Sullivan, too, thought highly of the story.

THE YEOMEN OF THE GUARD had its first performance at the Savoy Theatre on October 3, 1888. Both Gilbert and Sullivan considered it the best of all their operas.

ACT I ও⹀ The time was the sixteenth century. The place was the Tower of London. On the green within the walls a girl sat at her spinning wheel singing a plaintive song. She was Phoebe Meryll, daughter of Sergeant Meryll. Her father was a Yeoman of the Guard, stationed in the tower.

A man approached—Wilfred Shadbolt, head jailer in charge of the prisoners in the tower.

Phoebe received him coldly. She not only disliked him, but she was repelled by the duties he performed. Besides being head jailer, he was assistant tormentor of the prisoners.

Wilfred defended himself. He hadn't chosen his work because he liked it, he said. He added, with heavy sarcasm, "We can't *all* be sorcerers, you know."

The allusion was to Colonel Fairfax, a prisoner sentenced to die within the hour. He had been convicted of dealing with the devil.

"Colonel Fairfax is *not* a sorcerer," retorted Phoebe. "He's a man of science."

"Whatever he is, he won't be one long," said Wilfred.

She called him a monster for speaking so unfeelingly of the young and handsome soldier.

"Curse him!" said Wilfred in jealous rage.

Phoebe took up her spinning wheel and left.

A crowd of men and women came through the tower's grounds, followed by Yeomen of the Guard. The men and women moved on; the yeomen stayed. They were joined by Dame Carruthers, housekeeper to the tower. She spoke of

146

the poor prisoners, a dozen of whom were packed into one small cell. But Colonel Fairfax would be taken to another cell, she said, so that he might have his last hour alone with his confessor.

Phoebe had come back and was listening. She said warmly, "He's the bravest, the handsomest, and the best young gentleman in England. He twice saved my father's life, and it's a barbarous thing that so gallant a hero should lose his head."

After Dame Carruthers and the yeomen had gone, Phoebe remained on the green. Her father, Sergeant Meryll, found her there.

"Has no reprieve arrived for the poor gentleman?" she asked.

"No," said Meryll, "but there's hope yet. Your brother Leonard has been appointed a Yeoman of the Guard and will arrive today. As he comes straight from Windsor, where the court is, it may be that he will bring the reprieve with him."

But Leonard came without the reprieve. "I would I had brought better news," he said. "I'd give my life to save him."

"Do you speak in earnest?" asked his father.

"Aye," answered Leonard.

Sergeant Meryll had a desperate plan for saving Colonel Fairfax. Leonard had come to join the yeomen. No one had seen him enter the tower except a sentry who took little notice of him. "Lie hidden for a while," said his father. "I'll convey a yeoman's uniform to the colonel's cell—he shall shave off his beard so that none shall know him, and I'll own him as my son, the brave Leonard Meryll. He will be welcomed without question by my brother yeomen."

Wilfred Shadbolt was keeper of the keys. It would be Phoebe's task to get possession of the key to Fairfax' cell.

Leonard went away to wait in hiding. Phoebe saw guards leading Fairfax to another part of the prison. They came onto the green. Sir Richard Cholmondeley, Lieutenant of the Tower, was there to meet the colonel.

"I greet you with all good will," said Fairfax.

"You bear this bravely," said the lieutenant.

Phoebe was weeping. Her father took her away.

"And now, Sir Richard, I have a boon to ask," said Fairfax. He understood all too well why he was to die. His cousin, who was next in line to inherit the family estate, had charged him with sorcery. This cousin would be the sole heir, provided Fairfax died unmarried.

"As you will most surely do," said Sir Richard.

"As I will most surely *not* do," said Fairfax. "I have a mind to thwart my good cousin."

"How?" asked Sir Richard.

"By marriage, to be sure," answered Fairfax. He asked
Sir Richard to find him a bride—*any* bride who would marry
him in exchange for his dishonored name and a hundred
crowns besides.

Sir Richard promised to see what he could do, and Fairfax
was led away.

There was a sudden commotion outside. Two strolling
players rushed in, pursued by a crowd of men and women,
who demanded entertainment.

One of the players was Jack Point, a jester. The other
was Elsie Maynard, a singer. To quiet the ill-mannered
crowd, they sang and danced.

"A kiss for that, pretty maid!" shouted one of the men,
and he tried to kiss Elsie.

She called for help. Sir Richard gave a command, and his
guards cleared out the mob. "Now, my girl, who are you?"
he asked.

She told him that she and her partner were entertainers

who went from fair to fair, singing and dancing and making a poor living.

"Are you man and wife?" asked Sir Richard.

"No, sir," answered Jack Point. "Her mother travels with us, but the old woman is abed with fever, and we have come here to pick up some silver to buy medicine for her."

Sir Richard asked Elsie if she would like to earn a hundred crowns.

"A hundred crowns!" said Elsie. "They might save her life."

"Then listen," said Sir Richard. "A worthy gentleman is to be beheaded in an hour. For sufficient reasons he desires to marry before he dies. Will you be his wife?"

Jack Point intervened. "I am concerned in this. Though I am not yet wedded to Elsie Maynard, there's no knowing what may be in store for us. Have we your word that this gentleman will die today?"

Sir Richard gave his word.

"For my part, I consent," said Jack Point. "It is for Elsie to speak."

She, too, consented. Wilfred was summoned. He bound her eyes and conducted her into the tower.

"So you are a jester?" Sir Richard said to Jack Point. "I have a vacancy for such a one. What are your qualifications?"

The jester listed his qualifications, which were many, and the two men left to discuss the matter of employment.

Wilfred brought Elsie back from the tower and took the bandage from her eyes. As she went away, he eyed her curiously, wondering what business Lord Fairfax and his religious confessor could have had with a strange singing girl. He had tried to look into the cell, but they had stopped the keyhole.

Phoebe returned with her father. Meryll kept out of Wilfred's sight. She asked the jailer if Fairfax had yet been reprieved.

There was no reprieve, he answered; her adored Fairfax must die.

She insisted that she had only pity for the condemned man. She began to praise Wilfred for his cleverness and humor. All the while she was lifting the keys from his belt and passing them behind her to Meryll. He took them and disappeared into the tower.

Phoebe continued to flatter the jailer until her father brought back the keys. Without Wilfred's knowledge, she replaced them on his belt. Then, abruptly, she hurried off. He started after her.

Fairfax came out of the tower. He had shaved off his mustache and beard and was dressed in a yeoman's uniform. He said to Sergeant Meryll, who was waiting for him, "My good friend, you run a great risk for me."

"No risk. I warrant none here will recognize you," said Sergeant Meryll. "Now remember you are my brave son, Leonard Meryll."

Yeomen marched in to welcome the new member of the Guard. Phoebe entered with Wilfred close behind her. She threw her arms about Fairfax, crying, "My brother!"

"Aye, hug him, girl," said Wilfred. "There are three you may hug—your father and your brother and myself."

"And who are you?" asked Fairfax.

"We are betrothed," Wilfred told him importantly, and he commended Phoebe to her brother's care.

A bell tolled. People came crowding in to witness the execution. A block was set up, and the headsman took his place beside it. Sir Richard sent Wilfred, Fairfax, and two yeomen to bring out the prisoner.

The men returned in great excitement. The prisoner was not in his cell, they said.

Sir Richard ordered Wilfred arrested.

"I did not set him free," protested the jailer. "I hate the man."

Elsie and Jack Point were in the crowd.

"Oh, woe is me!" she whispered. "I am his wife, and he is free!"

"Oh, woe is *you*?" he returned bitterly. "Oh, woe is *me*, I rather think. You are his bride, and I am left alone!"

In a frenzy, the crowd and the yeomen scattered to hunt down the fugitive. Only the headsman, Elsie, and Fairfax were left behind. Elsie had fainted, and Fairfax held her in his arms.

ACT II ⧁ It was two days since the prisoner's disappearance. Yeomen of the Guard and a group of women had met in the moonlight on the tower green; they were discussing the mystery. Dame Carruthers and her niece Kate were there. Dame Carruthers taunted the men for having allowed Fairfax to escape. The other women took up the taunt, "Warders —whom do you ward?" as they all departed.

Jack Point and Wilfred Shadbolt met on the green. Both were in low spirits. Jack Point had been employed as Sir Richard's jester, but he found it hard to jest when his heart was broken. Wilfred had no employment at all. He had been dismissed for negligence of his duties.

He had often considered being a jester himself, he said; he thought it should not be difficult, seeing that Jack Point was one.

"Nothing easier," said Jack sardonically, and he touched on some of the hardships a professional humorist might have to bear. "My sweetheart, Elsie Maynard, was secretly wed to Fairfax half an hour before he escaped," he said. "While he lives, she is dead to me and I to her, so my jokes notwithstanding, I am the saddest dog in England!"

He made a reckless proposal to the former jailer. "If you will swear that you shot this Fairfax while he was trying to swim the river, and that he sank and was seen no more, I'll make you the very archbishop of jesters."

Wilfred hesitated. "Am I to lie?" he asked.

"Heartily," said Jack Point, and he promised to support the lie.

"And you will qualify me as a jester?" asked Wilfred.

Jack Point agreed to teach him all he had learned.

It was a bargain, said Wilfred, and they went away to concoct their story.

Fairfax came out of the tower, still disguised as a Yeoman of the Guard. Now that he was free, he regretted his hasty marriage. He wondered whom he had married. His bride was young, he thought, but he had not seen her face. Her features had been concealed by a blindfold.

Sergeant Meryll joined him.

Fairfax inquired after the health of Elsie Maynard.

"She is quite strong again and leaves us tonight," said Sergeant Meryll.

"Thanks to Dame Carruthers' kind nursing?" asked Fairfax.

Sergeant Meryll grimaced. "'Twas a sorry trick you played me, to bring the fainting girl to me. It gave the old lady an excuse for taking up quarters in my house. For the last two days I've shunned her like a plague. Another day of it and she would have married me!"

Dame Carruthers and her niece Kate approached. Dame Carruthers had something of importance to tell about Elsie Maynard. "She has a liking for you, Master Leonard," she said to Fairfax.

He was pleased. "She's as dainty a little maid as you'll find," he said.

"Then be warned in time, and give not your heart to her. *I* know what it is to give my heart to one who will have none of it," said Dame Carruthers, with a reproachful look at Sergeant Meryll.

"Why is my boy not to take heed of her?" asked Meryll. "She's a good girl."

"She's no girl," said Dame Carruthers. "She's a married woman." Her niece had overheard Elsie talking in her sleep. She had spoken of marrying someone she had never seen who was to die within an hour.

This was true, said Kate; she had written down all the words.

Dame Carruthers believed it was the escaped prisoner whom she had married.

After she, Kate, and Sergeant Meryll had gone, Fairfax reflected on his good fortune in having married Elsie. He might have found a far worse bride with his eyes open!

She was coming toward him. "Now to test her," he said to himself. It was not every husband who had the chance of courting his own wife.

"Mistress Elsie," he greeted her.

"Master Leonard," she said.

He asked her why she had fainted in his arms. Was it for joy at the news of Fairfax' escape?

"It may be so," she admitted.

Then, he said, he was jealous of this Colonel Fairfax. She was astonished.

"Shall I be frank?" he said. "I love you."

She was confused, not knowing what to say.

"Do you love me?" he asked.

"I am not free," she said. "I—I am a wife."

Fairfax demanded her husband's name.

She asked him to keep her secret. "My husband is none other than Colonel Fairfax."

Fairfax pretended indignation. "The greatest villain unhung!" he said.

"He is nothing to me—for I never saw him," said Elsie. "I was blindfolded, and he was to have died within the hour —and I am wedded to him—and my heart is broken!"

"Be mine. He will never know," said Fairfax. "Fly with me, Elsie. We will be married tomorrow."

"I *am* wed, and I have a duty," she said firmly. "Shame upon you!"

He tried to tell her he had spoken only to test her. The sound of a gunshot interrupted him.

Sergeant Meryll came running across the green. Men and women were hurrying after him. Sir Richard appeared, then Jack Point and Wilfred.

"Who fired the shot?" asked Sir Richard.

"It was I," said Wilfred. His story, corroborated by Jack Point, was that he had found Fairfax skulking in the vicinity of the tower. They had struggled; Fairfax had dived into the river; and Wilfred had shot him. The fugitive had been instantly killed, and his body had sunk like a lump of lead.

Wilfred was the hero of the hour. The crowd carried him off on their shoulders.

Elsie, Jack Point, Fairfax, and Phoebe stayed behind. Elsie had begun to weep. "Be comforted," said Jack Point. "Since he had to die, he might as well die thus."

"Still, he was my husband," she said, "and he was a brave man."

Fairfax asked Jack Point, "Are you sure it was Colonel Fairfax?"

"Aye," said the jester. He told Elsie, "You are free to choose again, so behold me. I am young. I have a pretty wit—"

Fairfax broke in. The jester did not know how to court a woman, he said. "Now listen to me." He spoke to Elsie, "There is one here who loves you well."

The jester stood by, listening. Phoebe listened too, and was alarmed as she saw Fairfax press Elsie's hand and whisper in her ear.

"Now that you are free, tell me," said Fairfax, "would you be the poor good fellow's wife?"

"I will be his true and loving wife," replied Elsie.

"My own dear love!" said Fairfax, taking her in his arms.

Now Jack Point realized how he had been tricked, and Phoebe burst into tears at seeing Fairfax lost to her.

Fairfax and Elsie left together. Jack Point went away alone. Phoebe stood weeping on the green.

Wilfred found her there and asked why she was in tears. She confessed that she wept for jealousy.

"I have not given you cause for jealousy," he said.

"Jealous of you? Bah!" she said fiercely. "I am jealous of another and a better man than you. And he is to marry Elsie Maynard, the little pale fool!"

Wilfred was staring at her. "The man you love is to marry Elsie Maynard? That is your brother, Leonard Meryll!"

Too late she realized how much she had revealed.

"You lying little jade!" he said in a fury. "Who is this man you have called brother? Should it be Fairfax? . . . It *is!* It's Fairfax—"

"Whom you have just shot through the head, and who lies at the bottom of the river!" she retorted.

He was taken aback. He began to stammer that he might have been mistaken.

He started to leave, and she stopped him. In her despair at losing Fairfax she said, "Whether he be or not, he is to marry Elsie, and—and I will be your wife!"

"Is that sure?" he asked eagerly.

"Aye, sure enough, for there's no help for it," she said. "You are a very brute, but even brutes must marry, I suppose."

The true Leonard Meryll suddenly appeared. "Phoebe, rejoice!" he called out. "I bring glad tidings!" Colonel Fairfax' reprieve had been signed two days ago, but it had been maliciously held back so that it would not arrive until after his death.

Beside herself with joy, Phoebe threw her arms about Leonard and kissed him.

Wilfred was raging. "Come away from him, you hussy! And as for you, sir, I'll skin you for this. Phoebe, who is this man?"

"Peace, fool," she said. "He is my brother."

He refused to believe her. "Another brother! Are there any more?"

This was the real Leonard Meryll, she told him. It was true that she had deceived him before, but she had done it only to save a prisoner's life. "Come, I am your Phoebe," she said wryly, "and we will be wed in a year—or two—or three."

Leonard had gone on to spread the word of Fairfax' reprieve. Sergeant Meryll came in to bring the news to Phoebe. He was startled to find her in Wilfred's arms.

"Oh, Father, he discovered our secret through my folly," she said, "and the price of his silence is—"

"Phoebe's heart," said Wilfred.

"Phoebe's *hand*," she corrected him.

"It's the same thing," he said.

"*Is* it?" she said, as he led her away.

Dame Carruthers had been eavesdropping. She had heard enough to convince her that it was the Merylls who had shielded Fairfax.

She threatened the sergeant. "A word from me, and three heads would roll besides his."

"Nay. Colonel Fairfax is reprieved," said Meryll. Yet he knew that even now it would be dangerous to reveal the part he had played in the colonel's escape. "Plague on the old meddler!" he muttered. But to her he said, "Here, pretty one. Such bloodthirsty words ill become those cherry lips."

She became melting and coy.

For many a month, he told her, he had been waiting to declare his love. "But never a word about Fairfax," he warned her. "The price of your silence is—"

"Meryll's heart," she said.

"No, Meryll's *hand*," he corrected her.

"It's the same thing," she said.

"*Is* it?" he said.

The yeomen marched in, accompanied by a crowd of women. They had come to the wedding.

Elsie was there, in bridal dress. Sir Richard delivered a message to her: "Your husband lives, and he is free and comes to claim his bride."

Elsie was stunned. "It cannot be!" she said.

Fairfax arrived, attended by other gentlemen. He said in a stern voice, "All thought of Leonard Meryll set aside. You are my own!"

In her heart, she bade good-by to the man she loved. Bowed with grief, she turned toward the husband who claimed her. She recognized him and cried out, realizing at last that the man she had known as Leonard Meryll was actually Fairfax.

Jack Point came slowly and sadly upon the scene. He saw the happiness about him. He began to sing the foolish little song he and Elsie had so often sung together. Then, as Elsie and Fairfax embraced, the jester fell insensible at their feet.

The Gondoliers

or

THE KING OF BARATARIA

◆§ *In the spring of 1889 Gilbert brought Sullivan a sketch of* THE GONDOLIERS. *Sullivan liked the story, and in spite of their past differences he and Gilbert worked smoothly together on the opera. It was first performed at the Savoy Theatre on December 7, 1889, and was one of their greatest successes.*

ACT I ❧ Venetian girls—Tessa and Gianetta among them
—had gathered on the piazzetta in front of the ducal palace
and were busily tying up bouquets of roses. A group of
gondoliers approached and asked whom the flowers were for.

"For Marco and Giuseppe Palmieri," replied the girls.
These two young men, handsomest and most charming of all
the gondoliers in Venice, would soon be here to choose
their brides.

Marco and Giuseppe rode up in a gondola, and the girls
filled their arms with roses. Both men declared that all the
prospective brides were so lovely that they could not possibly
choose among them. It was better, they decided, to let fate
make the choice. Their eyes were bandaged, and in a game
of blindman's buff Marco and Giuseppe each captured one
of the girls.

Giuseppe's bride, then, was to be Tessa. Marco's was to
be Gianetta.

Once the choices were made, the other girls waited no
longer. Each paired off with one of the other gondoliers,
and all hurried away to be married.

A gondola bearing the Duke and Duchess of Plaza-Toro
and their daughter, Casilda, drew up to the piazzetta. With
them was Luiz, their manservant. They had come from
Spain to pay an official visit to the Grand Inquisitor, and
impoverished though they were, they conducted themselves
with pompous dignity.

The duke was annoyed because no one was there to meet

them. He sent Luiz to the palace to inform the Grand Inquisitor of their arrival. As soon as the servant had gone, the duke told his daughter to prepare herself for a magnificent surprise.

It was a secret, said the duchess, which for state reasons had been kept for twenty years.

The duke told Casilda that when she was six months old she had been married by proxy to the infant son and heir of the wealthy King of Barataria. Shortly afterward the king had given up the religion of his ancestors and become a Wesleyan Methodist. To keep the alien religion from being handed down to the next generation, the Grand Inquisitor had had the king's son stolen and brought to Venice. A fortnight later the Methodist monarch and all his court perished in an uprising of the people.

"We are here to ascertain the whereabouts of your husband," said the duke, "and to hail you, our daughter, as Her Majesty, Queen of Barataria."

Luiz had returned. The duke and duchess left for the palace. The moment they were alone, Casilda and the servant rushed into each other's arms. In the presence of her parents she treated the young man disdainfully because of their difference in rank. Only in stolen moments could they express their true feelings.

But now Casilda quickly drew away from him. "I have embraced you for the last time," she said. "I have just learned that I was wed in babyhood to the infant son of the King of Barataria."

"The child who was stolen in infancy?" asked Luiz.

"The same," said Casilda. "But of course you know his story."

"Know his story?" said Luiz. "I have often told you that my mother was his nurse."

"True. I had forgotten," she said. "Well, he has been discovered, and my father has brought me here to claim his hand."

The duke and duchess came out of the palace with Don Alhambra del Bolero, the Grand Inquisitor. The duke introduced Don Alhambra as the man who had brought Casilda's infant husband to Venice.

166

"Unfortunately," said the duchess, "there appears to be some doubt as to His Majesty's whereabouts."

"Oh, dear, no—no doubt at all," said Don Alhambra. "I see him every day."

He told how he had taken the royal infant and left him with a gondolier, who had an infant son of his own. The two children were brought up together. The gondolier was given to drink, and after a while he became confused as to which child was which. The old gondolier died. The children followed his trade, so it was quite certain—beyond all probable, possible shadow of doubt—that the King of Barataria was a gondolier in Venice. Only one question remained —which of the two men was the king?

"You mean to say I am married to one of two gondoliers, but it is impossible to say which?" asked Casilda.

Don Alhambra tried to reassure her. The nurse who had cared for the royal child was the mother of their servant Luiz. She, no doubt, could establish the king's identity.

"How did you know that?" asked Luiz in surprise.

"A Grand Inquisitor is always up to date," said Don Alhambra smugly. He told Casilda that he was sending Luiz with two emissaries to his mother's address. "She will return with them," he said.

He conducted the duke and his family into the palace. Luiz departed in a gondola.

The gondoliers came back to the piazzetta with their brides. They celebrated joyfully until the Grand Inquisitor came out of the palace. His rather sinister appearance dampened their spirits. Two by two they drifted away, leaving only Marco and Giuseppe and their brides.

"Ceremony of some kind going on?" asked Don Alhambra.

The two couples answered that they had just been married.

"Now, my man," said Giuseppe, slapping Don Alhambra on the back, "if your curiosity's satisfied, you can go."

The Grand Inquisitor winced at this familiarity. "You must not call me your man. I don't think you know who I am."

Giuseppe neither knew nor cared. "We are the sons of Baptisto Palmieri, who led the last revolution," he said. "Republicans, heart and soul, we hold all men to be equal." He made it clear that he and his brother despised kings, rank, and wealth.

"How unfortunate," said Don Alhambra. "One of you may be Baptisto's son, but the other is no less than the only son of the last King of Barataria."

"One of us a *king*!" said Giuseppe.

"But which is it?" asked Marco.

"What does it matter?" returned Don Alhambra. Since they were both republicans and detested kings, of course they would give up all claim to the throne!

"When I say I detest kings, I mean *bad* kings," said Giuseppe hastily. He and Marco were able to think of many ways in which they could be the best of monarchs.

"Then we'll consider it settled," said Don Alhambra. Barataria was in a state of revolt. It was necessary that the king should take over the government at once. Until it could be established which of the gondoliers was king, they were to rule jointly.

"May we take our friends with us and give them places about the court?" asked Marco.

"Undoubtedly. That's always done," said Don Alhambra. But, he added, ladies were not admitted. Perhaps later they would be, but not at present.

The two couples were despondent at the thought of being separated, but they soon began to speculate on the glorious future in store for them. One of the brides would be queen and sit in a golden chair; noble lords would bow and scrape before her. Both Marco and Giuseppe would be king, government posts would be filled by their friends, and everyone would be equal.

The other gondoliers and their brides had come back to continue the celebration. Then a ship drew up to the quay, and there was weeping again, as farewells were said and the men sailed for Barataria.

169

ACT II 𝒆♥ Marco and Giuseppe were seated on two thrones in the court of Barataria. In the pavilion about them were the gondoliers' friends. Some were courtiers; others were servants or common soldiers. All mingled without regard for social distinction.

Marco and Giuseppe found their subjects lacking in respect and the servants little inclined to serve, but these were small matters. For the most part they considered themselves happy indeed.

"There's only one thing wanting to make us thoroughly comfortable," said Marco—"the wives we left behind us three months ago."

Giuseppe agreed that it *was* dull without female society. He and Marco were overjoyed when Tessa, Gianetta, and the other Venetian brides unexpectedly appeared. They had crossed the sea in a borrowed boat, they said, because they could no longer bear to be separated from their husbands.

They were full of questions about life in Barataria, and Gianetta wanted to know which of the two was king.

"We shan't know until the nurse turns up," said Giuseppe. A more important question to him was how to celebrate the ladies' arrival.

They began the festivities with a dance, which was interrupted by the arrival of Don Alhambra. Everyone fled except Marco and Giuseppe.

The Grand Inquisitor was astounded at what he had seen
—servants and noblemen dancing together. He told the
story of a wealthy king who wished that all his subjects
were as rich as he, so he gave everyone a high government
post and quickly learned a simple truth: where everyone is
somebody, then no one's anybody.

Gianetta and Tessa had stolen in to listen.

"Now I have some important news," said Don Alhambra.
"The Duke and Duchess of Plaza-Toro and their daughter,
Casilda, may be here at any moment."

Marco and Giuseppe replied that the duke and duchess
meant nothing to them.

"But the daughter—the beautiful daughter!" said Don Alhambra. "Oh, you're a lucky dog, one of you." He explained: many years ago either Marco or Giuseppe had married Casilda, who was now the loveliest young lady in Spain. Today she was here to claim one of them as her husband.

"We were married three months ago!" said Giuseppe in dismay.

"One of you—only one," said Don Alhambra. "The other is a bigamist."

Gianetta and Tessa made their presence known and pointed to themselves as the men's wives.

"Do you mean to say that one of these monarchs was already married?" demanded Gianetta.

"And that neither of us will be a queen?" asked Tessa.

"That is the idea," replied Don Alhambra.

The brides began to cry.

"Get away!" said Tessa, when Giuseppe came near her. "Perhaps it's you!"

"Don't!" said Gianetta, as Marco held out his arms to her. "Who knows whose husband you are?"

They would not be kept long in suspense, Don Alhambra assured them, and he left to speak with the woman who had nursed the royal child.

The two men and their brides considered their position. It appeared that Marco and Giuseppe had managed to acquire three wives. This was two-thirds of a husband to each wife.

But quiet, calm deliberation would untangle every knot, they told one another, and they went away to ponder the situation.

A train of attendants ceremoniously escorted the Duke and Duchess of Plaza-Toro and their daughter, Casilda, into the pavilion.

The duke told his daughter, "Prepare to receive the husband to whom you were united under such interesting circumstances."

"But which is it?" asked Casilda. "There are two of them."

The duke was certain that His Majesty would boil down to a single gentleman.

Casilda was resigned. Whatever happened she would be a dutiful wife, she promised, although she was sure she could never love her husband.

"I loved your father," said the duchess. "Several of my relatives bet me I couldn't, but I did."

Casilda hoped that when her husband saw what a shady family he had married into, he would break the marriage contract.

The duke was wounded by her attitude. He and the duchess acknowledged that they sometimes set a market value on their social position, but this was only making the most of their opportunities.

Marco and Giuseppe greeted the visitors, and the duke complained that he had not been welcomed with proper respect. He and his family gave Marco and Giuseppe a lesson in court etiquette. Then he and the duchess tactfully left the young people alone together.

"Gentlemen, I am bound to listen to you," said Casilda, "but it is right to tell you that I am in love with somebody else."

"Our case exactly," said Giuseppe. "*We* are in love with

somebody else. Our wives." He introduced Tessa and Gianetta.

Casilda tried to keep the arrangement from growing complicated, but the more they discussed it, the more confused it seemed to grow. The problem was still one of two husbands married to three brides.

Don Alhambra brought in the old woman who had cared for the infant prince. The Baratarian court assembled, along with the duke and duchess and their attendants. They waited for the nurse to speak.

She told how fondly she had guarded the prince. When kidnappers came she had substituted her own small son for the royal infant. The men had carried off her baby, leaving the prince, whom she had brought up as her son.

"His name—Luiz!" she announced. "Behold His Royal Highness."

The erstwhile servant came out of the crowd, wearing the crown and robes of a king. He ascended the throne.

Casilda flung herself into Luiz' arms, and the king and his high-born bride were acclaimed.

Tessa and Gianetta, although a little sad at giving up all hope of being a queen, were happy to be reunited with their husbands. And Marco and Giuseppe were happy at the prospect of returning with their wives to Venice, where they would be simple gondoliers again.

Selected Lyrics
from
Gilbert and Sullivan Operas

TRIAL BY JURY

SONG—EDWIN

When first my old, old love I knew,
  My bosom welled with joy;
My riches at her feet I threw—
  I was a love-sick boy!
No terms seemed too extravagant
  Upon her to employ—
I used to mope and sigh and pant,
  Just like a love-sick boy!
            Tink-a-tank, tink-a-tank.

But joy incessant palls the sense;
    And love, unchanged, will cloy,
And she became a bore intense
    Unto her love-sick boy!
With fitful glimmer burnt my flame,
    And I grew cold and coy,
At last, one morning, I became
    Another's love-sick boy.
                  Tink-a-tank, tink-a-tank.

SONG—JUDGE

When I, good friends, was called to the bar,
    I'd an appetite fresh and hearty,
But I was, as many young barristers are,
    An impecunious party.
I'd a swallow-tail coat of a beautiful blue—
    A brief which I bought of a booby—
A couple of shirts and a collar or two,
    And a ring that looked like a ruby!

In Westminster Hall I danced a dance,
    Like a semi-despondent fury;
For I thought I should never hit on a chance
    Of addressing a British jury.
But I soon got tired of third-class journeys,
    And dinners of bread and water;
So I fell in love with a rich attorney's
    Elderly, ugly daughter.

The rich attorney, he jumped with joy,
    And replied to my fond professions:
"You shall reap the reward of your pluck, my boy,
    At the Bailey and Middlesex Sessions.
You'll soon get used to her looks," said he,
    "And a very nice girl you'll find her.
She may very well pass for forty-three
    In the dusk, with a light behind her!"

The rich attorney was good as his word;
    The briefs came trooping gaily,

And every day my voice was heard
  At the Sessions or Ancient Bailey.
All thieves who could my fees afford
  Relied on my orations,
And many a burglar I've restored
  To his friends and his relations.

At length I became as rich as the Gurneys—
  An incubus then I thought her,
So I threw over that rich attorney's
  Elderly, ugly daughter.
The rich attorney my character high
  Tried vainly to disparage—
And now, if you please, I'm ready to try
  This breach of promise of marriage!

SONG—COUNSEL FOR THE PLAINTIFF

With a sense of deep emotion
  I approach this painful case;
For I never had a notion
  That a man could be so base,
Or deceive a girl confiding,
Vows, *etcetera*, deriding.

See my interesting client,
  Victim of a heartless wile!
See the traitor all defiant
  Wear a supercilious smile!
Sweetly smiled my client on him,
Coyly woo'd and gently won him.

. . . . .

Picture, then, my client naming
  And insisting on the day:
Picture him excuses framing—
  Going from her far away;
Doubly criminal to do so,
For the maid had bought her *trousseau!*

SONG—EDWIN

Oh, gentlemen, listen, I pray,
    Though I own that my heart has been ranging,
Of nature the laws I obey,
    For nature is constantly changing.
The moon in her phases is found,
    The time and the wind and the weather,
The months in succession come round,
    And you don't find two Mondays together.
Consider the moral, I pray,
    Nor bring a young fellow to sorrow,
Who loves this young lady today,
    And loves that young lady tomorrow.

You cannot eat breakfast all day,
    Nor is it the act of a sinner,
When breakfast is taken away,
    To turn his attention to dinner;
And it's not in the range of belief,
    That you could hold him as a glutton,
Who, when he is tired of beef,
    Determines to tackle the mutton.
But this I am willing to say,
    If it will appease her sorrow,
I'll marry this lady today,
    And I'll marry that lady tomorrow!

THE SORCERER

ACT I

SONG—DR. DALY

Time was when Love and I were well acquainted.
    Time was when we walked ever hand in hand.
A saintly youth with worldly thought untainted,

None better loved than I in all the land!
Time was, when maidens of the noblest station,
  Forsaking even military men,
Would gaze upon me, rapt in adoration—
  Ah me, I was a fair young curate then!

Had I a headache? sighed the maids assembled;
  Had I a cold? welled forth the silent tear;
Did I look pale? then half a parish trembled;
  And when I coughed all thought the end was near!
I had no care—no jealous doubts hung o'er me—
  For I was loved beyond all other men.
Fled gilded dukes and belted earls before me—
  Ah me, I was a pale young curate then!

SONG—MR. WELLS

My name is John Wellington Wells,
I'm a dealer in magic and spells,
  In blessings and curses
  And ever-filled purses,
In prophecies, witches, and knells.

If you want a proud foe to make tracks—
If you'd melt a rich uncle in wax—
  You've but to look in
  On our resident Djinn,
Number seventy, Simmery Axe!

We've a first-class assortment of magic;
  And for raising a posthumous shade
With effects that are comic or tragic,
  There's no cheaper house in the trade.
Love-philtre—we've quantities of it;
  And for knowledge if anyone burns,
We keep an extremely small prophet, a prophet
  Who brings us unbounded returns:

  For he can prophesy
  With a wink of his eye,
  Peep with security

Into futurity,
Sum up your history,
Clear up a mystery,
Humor proclivity
For a nativity—for a nativity;
He has answers oracular,
Bogies spectacular,
Tetrapods tragical,
Mirrors so magical,
Answers oracular,
Facts astronomical,
Solemn or comical,
And, if you want it, he
Makes a reduction on taking a quantity!
  Oh!

If anyone anything lacks,
He'll find it all ready in stacks,
  If he'll only look in
  On the resident Djinn,
Number seventy, Simmery Axe!

He can raise you hosts
Of ghosts,
And that without reflectors;
And creepy things
With wings,
And gaunt and grisly spectres.
He can fill you crowds
Of shrouds,
And horrify you vastly;
He can rack your brains
With chains,
And gibberings grim and ghastly!

Then, if you plan it, he
Changes organity,
With an urbanity
Full of Satanity,
Vexes humanity

With an inanity
Fatal to vanity—
Driving your foes to the verge of insanity!

Barring tautology,
In demonology,
'Lectro-biology,
Mystic nosology,
Spirit philology,
High-class astrology,
Such is his knowledge, he
Isn't the man to require an apology!
   Oh!

My name is John Wellington Wells,
I'm a dealer in magic and spells,
  In blessings and curses
  And ever-filled purses,
In prophecies, witches, and knells.

If anyone anything lacks,
He'll find it all ready in stacks,
  If he'll only look in
  On the resident Djinn,
Number seventy, Simmery Axe!

ACT II

SONG——CONSTANCE

Dear friends, take pity on my lot,
  My cup is not of nectar!
I long have loved—as who would not?—
  Our kind and reverend rector.
Long years ago my love began
  So sweetly—yet so sadly—
But when I saw this plain old man,
Away my old affection ran—
  I found I loved him madly.
    Oh!

I know not why I love him so;
　It is enchantment, surely!
He's dry and snuffy, deaf and slow,
　Ill-tempered, weak, and poorly!
He's ugly, and absurdly dressed,
　And sixty-seven nearly,
He's everything that I detest,
But if the truth must be confessed,
　I love him very dearly!
　　Oh!

DUET—MR. WELLS *and* LADY SANGAZURE

MR. W.	Hate me! I drop my H's—have through life!
LADY S.	Love me! I'll drop them, too!
MR. W.	Hate me! I always eat peas with a knife!
LADY S.	Love me! I'll eat like you!
MR. W.	Hate me! I spend the day at Rosherville!
LADY S.	Love me! that joy I'll share!
MR. W.	Hate me! I often roll down One Tree Hill!
LADY S.	Love me! I'll join you there!
LADY S.	Love me! my prejudices I will drop!
MR. W.	Hate me! that's not enough!
LADY S.	Love me! I'll come and help you in the shop!
MR. W.	Hate me! the life is rough!
LADY S.	Love me! my grammar I will all forswear!
MR. W.	Hate me! abjure my lot!
LADY S.	Love me! I'll stick sunflowers in my hair!
MR. W.	Hate me! they'll suit you not!
MR. W.	At what I am going to say be not enraged—
	I may not love you—for I am engaged!

H.M.S. PINAFORE

ACT I

We sail the ocean blue,
And our saucy ship's a beauty;
We're sober men and true,
And attentive to our duty.
When the balls whistle free
O'er the bright blue sea,
We stand to our guns all day;
When at anchor we ride
On the Portsmouth tide,
We have plenty of time to play.

SONG—LITTLE BUTTERCUP

For I'm called Little Buttercup—dear little Buttercup,
  Though I could never tell why,
But still I'm called Buttercup—poor little Buttercup,
  Sweet Little Buttercup I!

I've snuff and tobaccy, and excellent jacky,
  I've scissors and watches and knives;
I've ribbons and laces to set off the faces
  Of pretty young sweethearts and wives.

I've treacle and toffee, I've tea and I've coffee,
  Soft tommy and succulent chops;
I've chickens and conies, and pretty polonies,
  And excellent peppermint drops.

Then buy of your Buttercup—dear Little Buttercup;
  Sailors should never be shy;
So buy of your Buttercup—poor Little Buttercup;
  Come, of your Buttercup buy!

SONG—RALPH

A maiden fair to see,
The pearl of minstrelsy,
  A bud of blushing beauty;
For whom proud nobles sigh,
And with each other vie
  To do her menial's duty.

A suitor, lowly born,
With hopeless passion torn,
  And poor beyond denying,
Has dared for her to pine
At whose exalted shrine
  A world of wealth is sighing.

Unlearned he in aught
Save that which love has taught
  (For love has been his tutor);
Oh, pity, pity me—
Our captain's daughter she,
  And I that lowly suitor!

SONG—CAPTAIN CORCORAN *and* CREW

CAPT. I am the captain of the *Pinafore;*
CREW And a right good captain, too!
CAPT.   You're very, very good,
    And be it understood,
  I command a right good crew.
CREW   We're very, very good,
    And be it understood,
  He commands a right good crew.
CAPT.   Though related to a peer,
    I can hand, reef, and steer,
  And ship a selvagee;
    I am never known to quail
    At the fury of a gale,
  And I'm never, never sick at sea!
CREW   What, never?
CAPT.   No, never!

CREW	What, *never?*
CAPT.	Hardly ever!
CREW	He's hardly ever sick at sea!
	Then give three cheers and one cheer more
	For the hardy Captain of the *Pinafore!*

CAPT.	I do my best to satisfy you all—
CREW	And with you we're quite content.
CAPT.	You're exceedingly polite,
	And I think it only right
	To return the compliment.
CREW	We're exceedingly polite,
	And he thinks it's only right
	To return the compliment.
CAPT.	Bad language or abuse,
	I never, never use,
	Whatever the emergency;
	Though "Bother it," I may
	Occasionally say,
	I never use a big, big D.
CREW	What, never?
CAPT.	No, never!
CREW	What, *never?*
CAPT.	Hardly ever!
CREW	Hardly ever swears a big, big D—
	Then give three cheers and one cheer more
	For the well-bred Captain of the *Pinafore!*

SONG—SIR JOSEPH PORTER

When I was a lad I served a term
As office boy to an attorney's firm.
I cleaned the windows and I swept the floor,
And I polished up the handle of the big front door.
    I polished up that handle so carefullee,
        That now I am the Ruler of the Queen's Navee!

As office boy I made such a mark
That they gave me the post of a junior clerk.

I served the writs with a smile so bland,
And I copied all the letters in a big round hand—
    I copied all the letters in a hand so free,
      That now I am the Ruler of the Queen's Navee!

In serving writs I made such a name
That an articled clerk I soon became;
I wore clean collars and a brand-new suit
For the pass examination at the Institute,
    And that pass examination did so well for me,
      That now I am the Ruler of the Queen's Navee!

       · · · ·

I grew so rich that I was sent
By a pocket borough into Parliament.
I always voted at my party's call,
And I never thought of thinking for myself at all.
    I thought so little, they rewarded me
      By making me the Ruler of the Queen's Navee!

Now landsmen all, whoever you may be,
If you want to rise to the top of the tree,
If your soul isn't fettered to an office stool,
Be careful to be guided by this golden rule—
    Stick close to your desks and never go to sea,
      And you all may be Rulers of the Queen's Navee!

DUET—JOSEPHINE and RALPH

JOS.
    Refrain, audacious tar,
      Your suit from pressing,
    Remember what you are,
      And whom addressing!

(*Aside*)
    I'd laugh my rank to scorn
      In union holy,
    Were he more highly born
      Or I more lowly!

RALPH
    Proud lady, have your way,
      Unfeeling beauty!
    You speak and I obey,

It is my duty!
I am the lowliest tar
   That sails the water,
And you, proud maiden, are
   My captain's daughter!
(*Aside*)   My heart with anguish torn
   Bows down before her,
She laughs my love to scorn,
   Yet I adore her!

ACT II

SONG—CAPTAIN CORCORAN

Fair moon, to thee I sing,
   Bright regent of the heavens,
Say, why is everything
   Either at sixes or at sevens?
I have lived hitherto
   Free from breath of slander,
Beloved by all my crew—
   A really popular commander.
But now my kindly crew rebel,
   My daughter to a tar is partial,
Sir Joseph storms, and, sad to tell,
   He threatens a court martial!
Fair moon, to thee I sing,
   Bright regent of the heavens,
Say, why is everything
   Either at sixes or at sevens?

DUET—LITTLE BUTTERCUP *and* CAPTAIN CORCORAN

BUT.   Things are seldom what they seem,
   Skim milk masquerades as cream;
   Highlows pass as patent leathers;
   Jackdaws strut in peacock's feathers.
CAPT. (*puzzled*)   Very true,

	So they do.
BUT.	Black sheep dwell in every fold;
	All that glitters is not gold;
	Storks turn out to be but logs;
	Bulls are but inflated frogs.
CAPT. (*puzzled*)	So they be,
	Frequentlee.
BUT.	Drops the wind and stops the mill;
	Turbot is ambitious brill;
	Gild the farthing if you will,
	Yet it is a farthing still.
CAPT. (*puzzled*)	Yes, I know.
	That is so.
	Though to catch your drift I'm striving,
	It is shady—it is shady;
	I don't see at what you're driving,
	Mystic lady—mystic lady.
(*Aside*)	Stern conviction's o'er me stealing,
	That the mystic lady's dealing
	In oracular revealing.
BUT. (*aside*)	Stern conviction's o'er him stealing,
	That the mystic lady's dealing
	In oracular revealing.
BOTH	Yes, I know—
	That is so!
CAPT.	Though I'm anything but clever,
	I could talk like that forever:
	Once a cat was killed by care;
	Only brave deserve the fair.
BUT.	Very true,
	So they do.
CAPT.	Wink is often good as nod;
	Spoils the child who spares the rod;
	Thirsty lambs run foxy dangers;
	Dogs are found in many mangers.
BUT.	Frequentlee,
	I agree.
CAPT.	Paw of cat the chestnut snatches;

Worn-out garments show new patches;
Only count the chick that hatches;
Men are grown-up catchy-catchies.

BUT.
              Yes, I know,
              That is so.

(*Aside*)
Though to catch my drift he's striving,
    I'll dissemble—I'll dissemble;
When he sees at what I'm driving,
    Let him tremble—let him tremble!

BOTH
Though a mystic tone $\left\{ \begin{matrix} \text{I} \\ \text{you} \end{matrix} \right\}$ borrow,

$\left. \begin{matrix} \text{You will} \\ \text{I shall} \end{matrix} \right\}$ learn the truth with sorrow,

Here today and gone tomorrow;
        Yes, I know—
        That is so!

TRIO—CAPTAIN CORCORAN, SIR JOSEPH PORTER, *and* JOSEPHINE

CAPT.
Never mind the why and wherefore,
Love can level ranks, and therefore,
Though his lordship's station's mighty,
    Though stupendous be his brain,
Though your tastes are mean and flighty
    And your fortune poor and plain,

CAPT. *and*
SIR JOSEPH
Ring the merry bells on board ship,
    Rend the air with warbling wild,

For the union of $\left\{ \begin{matrix} \text{his} \\ \text{my} \end{matrix} \right\}$ lordship

    With a humble captain's child!

CAPT.   For a humble captain's daughter—
JOS.   For a gallant captain's daughter—
SIR JOSEPH   And a lord who rules the water—
JOS. (*aside*) And a *tar* who ploughs the water!

ALL
Let the air with joy be laden,
    Rend with songs the air above,
For the union of a maiden
    With the man who owns her love!

SIR JOSEPH
Never mind the why and wherefore,

Love can level ranks, and therefore,
Though your nautical relation
  In my set could scarcely pass—
Though you occupy a station
  In the lower middle class—

CAPT. *and*   Ring the merry bells on board ship,
SIR JOSEPH   Rend the air with warbling wild,

For the union of $\left\{\begin{array}{c} \text{my} \\ \text{his} \end{array}\right\}$ lordship

  With a humble captain's child!

CAPT.   For a humble captain's daughter—
JOS.   For a gallant captain's daughter—
SIR JOSEPH   And a lord who rules the water—
JOS. (*aside*)   And a *tar* who ploughs the water!
ALL   Let the air with joy be laden,
  Rend with songs the air above,
For the union of a maiden
  With the man who owns her love!

JOS.   Never mind the why and wherefore,
Love can level ranks, and therefore
I admit the jurisdiction;
  Ably you have played your part;
You have carried firm conviction
  To my hesitating heart.

CAPT. *and*   Ring the merry bells on board ship,
SIR JOSEPH   Rend the air with warbling wild,

For the union of $\left\{\begin{array}{c} \text{my} \\ \text{his} \end{array}\right\}$ lordship

  With a humble captain's child!

CAPT.   For a humble captain's daughter—
JOS.   For a gallant captain's daughter—
SIR JOSEPH   And a lord who rules the water—
JOS. (*aside*)   And a *tar* who ploughs the water!
(*Aloud*)   Let the air with joy be laden.
CAPT., SIR JOSEPH Ring the merry bells on board ship—
JOS.   For the union of a maiden—
CAPT., SIR JOSEPH For her union with his lordship.
ALL   Rend with songs the air above
For the man who owns her love!

SCENE—RALPH, JOSEPHINE, BOATSWAIN, *and* CREW

RALPH *and* JOS. I,
He, } humble, poor, and lowly born,
The meanest in the port division—
The butt of epauletted scorn—
The mark of quarter-deck derision—
Have
Has } dared to raise { my
his } wormy eyes
Above the dust to which you'd mould { me
him
In manhood's glorious pride to rise,
I am
He is } an Englishman—behold { me!
him!

CREW He is an Englishman!
BOAT. He is an Englishman!
For he himself has said it,
And it's greatly to his credit,
That he is an Englishman!

CREW That he is an Englishman!
BOAT. For he might have been a Roosian,
A French or Turk or Proosian,
Or perhaps Itali-an!

CREW Or perhaps Itali-an!
BOAT. But in spite of all temptations
To belong to other nations,
He remains an Englishman!

SONG—LITTLE BUTTERCUP *and* CHORUS

BUT. A many years ago,
    When I was young and charming,
As some of you may know,
    I practiced baby-farming.

CHO. Now this is most alarming!
    When she was young and charming,
She practiced baby-farming,
    A many years ago.

BUT. Two tender babes I nussed:

One was of low condition,
The other, upper crust,
A regular patrician.

CHO.   Now this is the position:
One was of low condition,
The other a patrician,
A many years ago.

BUT.   Oh, bitter is my cup!
However could I do it?
I mixed those children up,
And not a creature knew it!

CHO.   However could you do it?
Some day, no doubt, you'll rue it,
Although no creature knew it,
So many years ago.

BUT.   In time each little waif
Forsook his foster-mother,
The well-born babe was Ralph—
Your captain was the other!

CHO.   They left their foster-mother,
The one was Ralph, our brother,
Our captain was the other,
A many years ago.

THE PIRATES OF PENZANCE

ACT I

SONG—RUTH

When Frederic was a little lad he proved so brave and daring,
His father thought he'd 'prentice him to some career seafaring.
I was, alas, his nurserymaid, and so it fell to *my* lot

To take and bind the promising boy apprentice to a *pilot*—
A life not bad for a hardy lad, though surely not a high lot,
Though I'm a nurse, you might do worse than make your boy a pilot.

I was a stupid nurserymaid, on breakers always steering,
And I did not catch the word aright, through being hard of hearing;
Mistaking my instructions, which within my brain did gyrate,
I took and bound this promising boy apprentice to a *pirate*.
A sad mistake it was to make and doom him to a vile lot.
I bound him to a pirate—you—instead of to a pilot.

I soon found out, beyond all doubt, the scope of this disaster,
But I hadn't the face to return to my place and break it to my master.
A nurserymaid is not afraid of what you people *call* work,
So I made up my mind to go as a kind of piratical maid-of-all-work.
And that is how you find me now, a member of your shy lot,
Which you wouldn't have found, had he been bound apprentice to a
    pilot.

SONG—PIRATE KING *and* CHORUS

KING   Oh, better far to live and die
                    Under the brave, black flag I fly,
                    Than play a sanctimonious part,
                    With a pirate head and a pirate heart.
                    Away to the cheating world go you,
                    Where pirates all are well-to-do;
                    But I'll be true to the song I sing,
                    And live and die a pirate king.
                        For I am a pirate king.

CHO.   You are!
                    Hurrah for our pirate king!

KING   And it is, it is a glorious thing
                    To be a pirate king.

CHO.   Hurrah!
                    Hurrah for our pirate king!

KING   When I sally forth to seek my prey,
                    I help myself in a royal way:
                    I sink a few more ships, it's true,
                    Than a well-bred monarch ought to do;

But many a king on a first-class throne,
If he wants to call his crown his own,
Must manage somehow to get through
More dirty work than ever *I* do,
    Though I am a pirate king.
CHO.   You are!
Hurrah for our pirate king!
KING   And it is, it is a glorious thing
    To be a pirate king!
CHO.   It is!
Hurrah for our pirate king!

SONG—FREDERIC *and* CHORUS

FRED.   Oh, is there not one maiden breast
    Which does not feel the moral beauty
Of making worldly interest
    Subordinate to sense of duty?
Who would not give up willingly
    All matrimonial ambition
To rescue such a one as I
    From his unfortunate position?

CHO.   Alas! there's not one maiden breast
    Which seems to feel the moral beauty
Of making worldly interest
    Subordinate to sense of duty!

FRED.   Oh, is there not one maiden here
    Whose homely face and bad complexion
Have caused all hopes to disappear
    Of ever winning man's affection?
To such a one, if such there be,
    I swear by heaven's arch above you,
If you will cast your eyes on me—
    However plain you be—I'll love you!

CHO.   Alas! there's not one maiden here
    Whose homely face and bad complexion
Have caused all hope to disappear
    Of ever winning man's affection!

SONG—MABEL *and* CHORUS

Poor wandering one!
Though thou hast surely strayed,
  Take heart of grace,
  Thy steps retrace,
Poor wandering one!

Poor wandering one!
If such poor love as mine
  Can help thee find
  True peace of mind—
Why, take it, it is thine!

CHO.   Take heart, no danger lowers;
            Take any heart—but ours!

MABEL   Take heart, fair days will shine;
            Take any heart—take mine!

SONG—MAJOR-GENERAL

I am the very model of a modern Major-General,
I've information vegetable, animal, and mineral,
I know the kings of England, and I quote the fights historical,
From Marathon to Waterloo, in order categorical;
I'm very well acquainted too with matters mathematical,
I understand equations, both the simple and quadratical,
About binomial theorem I'm teeming with a lot o' news—
With many cheerful facts about the square of the hypotenuse.

I'm very good at integral and differential calculus,
I know the scientific names of beings animalculous;
In short, in matters vegetable, animal, and mineral,
I am the very model of a modern Major-General.

I know our mythic history, King Arthur's and Sir Caradoc's,
I answer hard acrostics, I've a pretty taste for paradox,
I quote in elegiacs all the crimes of Heliogabalus,
In conics I can floor peculiarities parabolous.
I can tell undoubted Raphaels from Gerard Dows and Zoffanies,
I know the croaking chorus from the *Frogs* of Aristophanes,

Then I can hum a fugue of which I've heard the music's din afore,
And whistle all the airs from that infernal nonsense *Pinafore*.

Then I can write a washing bill in Babylonic cuneiform,
And tell you every detail of Caractacus's uniform;
In short, in matters vegetable, animal, and mineral,
I am the very model of a modern Major-General.

.   .   .   .   .

ACT II

SCENE—SERGEANT, POLICEMEN, MABEL, EDITH, *and* SISTERS

SERG.
 When the foeman bares his steel,
   Tarantara, tarantara!
 We uncomfortable feel,
   Tarantara!
 And we find the wisest thing,
   Tarantara, tarantara!
 Is to slap our chests and sing
   Tarantara!
 For when threatened with emeutes,
   Tarantara, tarantara!
 And your heart is in your boots,
   Tarantara!
 There is nothing brings it round,
   Tarantara, tarantara!
 Like the trumpet's martial sound,
   Tarantara, tarantara!
 Tarantara-ra-ra-ra-ra!

POLICE
 Tarantara-ra-ra-ra-ra!

MABEL
 Go, ye heroes, go to glory,
 Though you die in combat gory,
 Ye shall live in song and story.
   Go to immortality!
 Go to death, and go to slaughter;

Die and every Cornish daughter
With her tears your grave shall water.
Go, ye heroes, go and die!

GIRLS
Go, ye heroes, go and die!

POLICE
Though to us it's evident,
Tarantara, tarantara!
These intentions are well meant,
Tarantara!
Such expressions don't appear,
Tarantara, tarantara!
Calculated men to cheer,
Tarantara!
Who are going to meet their fate
In a highly nervous state,
Tarantara!
Still to us it's evident
These intentions are well meant.
Tarantara!

EDITH
Go and do your best endeavor,
And before all links we sever,
We will say farewell forever.
Go to glory and the grave!

GIRLS
For your foes are fierce and ruthless,
False, unmerciful, and truthless.
Young and tender, old and toothless,
All in vain their mercy crave.

SERG.
We observe too great a stress,
On the risks that on us press,
And of reference a lack
To our chance of coming back.
Still, perhaps it would be wise
Not to carp or criticise,
For it's very evident
These attentions are well meant.

GIRLS
Yes, to them it's evident
Our attentions are well meant.
Tarantara-ra-ra-ra-ra!

SONG—SERGEANT

When a felon's not engaged in his employment,
Or maturing his felonious little plans,
His capacity for innocent enjoyment
Is just as great as any honest man's.
Our feelings we with difficulty smother,
When constabulary duty's to be done.
Ah, take one consideration with another,
A policeman's lot is not a happy one.

When the enterprising burglar's not a-burgling,
When the cut-throat isn't occupied in crime,
He loves to hear the little brook a-gurgling
And listen to the merry village chime.
When the coster's finished jumping on his mother,
He loves to lie a-basking in the sun.
Ah, take one consideration with another,
The policeman's lot is not a happy one.

PATIENCE

ACT I

SONG—BUNTHORNE

If you're anxious for to shine in the high aesthetic line as a man of
    culture rare,
You must get up all the germs of the transcendental terms, and plant
    them everywhere.
You must lie upon the daisies and discourse in novel phrases of your
    complicated state of mind,
The meaning doesn't matter if it's only idle chatter of a transcendental
    kind.

            And everyone will say,
            As you walk your mystic way,

"If this young man expresses himself in terms too deep for *me*,
Why, what a very singularly deep young man this deep young man
    must be!"

          .   .   .   .   .

Then a sentimental passion of a vegetable fashion must excite your
    languid spleen,
An attachment *à la* Plato for a bashful young potato, or a
    not-too-French French bean!
Though the Philistines may jostle, you will rank as an apostle in the
    high aesthetic band,
If you walk down Piccadilly with a poppy or a lily in your
    medieval hand.
           And everyone will say,
           As you walk your flowery way,
"If he's content with a vegetable love which would certainly not
    suit *me*,
Why, what a most particularly pure young man this pure young
    man must be!"

DUET—PATIENCE *and* ANGELA

PA.   Long years ago—fourteen, maybe—
               When but a tiny babe of four,
           Another baby played with me,
               My elder by a year or more;
           A little child of beauty rare,
           With marvellous eyes and wondrous hair,
           Who, in my child-eyes, seemed to me
           All that a little child should be!
               Ah, how we loved, that child and I!
                 How pure our baby joy!
               How true our love—and, by the by,
                 He was a little boy!

ANG.   Ah, old, old tale of Cupid's touch!
           I thought as much—I thought as much!
               He *was* a little boy!
PA.   Pray don't misconstrue what I say—
           Remember, pray—remember, pray—

He was a *little* boy!

ANG.   No doubt! Yet, spite of all your pains,
The interesting fact remains—
He was a little *boy!*

DUET—GROSVENOR *and* PATIENCE

GROS.   Prithee, pretty maiden—prithee, tell me true,
(Hey, but I'm doleful, willow willow waly!)
Have you e'er a lover a-dangling after you?
Hey willow waly O!
I would fain discover
If you have a lover.
Hey willow waly O!

PA.   Gentle sir, my heart is frolicsome and free—
(Hey, but he's doleful, willow willow waly!)
Nobody I care for comes a-courting me—
Hey willow waly O!
Nobody I care for
Comes a-courting—therefore,
Hey willow waly O!

GROS.   Prithee, pretty maiden, will you marry me?
(Hey, but I'm hopeful, willow willow waly!)
I may say at once I'm a man of propertee—
Hey willow waly O!
Money, I despise it;
Many people prize it,
Hey willow waly O!

PA.   Gentle sir, although to marry I design—
(Hey, but he's hopeful, willow willow waly!)
As yet I do not know you, and so I must decline.
Hey willow waly O!
To other maidens go you—
As yet I do not know you,
Hey willow waly O!

ACT II

SONG—LADY JANE

Silvered is the raven hair,
    Spreading is the parting straight,
Mottled the complexion fair,
    Halting is the youthful gait,
Hollow is the laughter free,
    Spectacled the limpid eye—
Little will be left of me
    In the coming by and by!

Fading is the taper waist,
    Shapeless grows the shapely limb,
And although severely laced,
    Spreading is the figure trim!
Stouter than I used to be,
    Still more corpulent grow I—
There will be too much of me
    In the coming by and by!

SONG—GROSVENOR

A magnet hung in a hardware shop,
And all around was a loving crop
Of scissors and needles, nails and knives,
Offering love for all their lives;
But for iron the magnet felt no whim,
Though he charmed iron, it charmed not him;
From needles and nails and knives he'd turn,
For he'd set his love on a silver churn!
        His most aesthetic,
        Very magnetic
    Fancy took this turn—
        "If I can wheedle
        A knife or a needle,
    Why not a silver churn?"

And iron and steel expressed surprise,

The needles opened their well-drilled eyes,
The penknives felt "shut up," no doubt,
The scissors declared themselves "cut out,"
The kettles they boiled with rage, 'tis said,
While every nail went off its head,
And hither and thither began to roam,
Till a hammer came up—and drove them home.
        While this magnetic,
        Peripatetic
    Lover he lived to learn,
        By no endeavor
        Can a magnet ever
    Attract a silver churn!

DUET—BUNTHORNE *and* GROSVENOR

BUN. When I go out of door,
    Of damozels a score
        (All sighing and burning,
        And clinging and yearning)
    Will follow me as before.
    I shall, with cultured taste,
    Distinguish gems from paste,
        And "High diddle diddle"
        Will rank as an idyll,
    If I pronounce it chaste!

BOTH   A most intense young man,
        A soulful-eyed young man,
    An ultra-poetical, super-aesthetical,
        Out-of-the-way young man!

GROS. Conceive me, if you can,
    An every-day young man:
        A commonplace type,
        With a stick and a pipe,
    And a half-bred black-and-tan;
    Who thinks suburban "hops"
    More fun than "Monday Pops,"
        Who's fond of his dinner

And doesn't get thinner
On bottled beer and chops.

BOTH   A commonplace young man,
A matter-of-fact young man,
A steady and stolid-y, jolly bank-holiday
Every-day young man!

BUN.   A Japanese young man,
A blue-and-white young man,
Francesca da Rimini, miminy, piminy,
Je-ne-sais-quoi young man!

GROS.   A Chancery Lane young man,
A Somerset House young man,
A very delectable, highly respectable,
Threepenny-bus young man!

BUN.   A pallid and thin young man,
A haggard and lank young man,
A greenery-yallery, Grosvenor Gallery,
Foot-in-the-grave young man!

GROS.   A Sewell & Cross young man,
A Howell & James young man,
A pushing young particle—"What's the next article?"—
Waterloo-House young man!

BUN.   Conceive me, if you can,
A crotchety, cracked young man,
An ultra-poetical, super-aesthetical,
Out-of-the-way young man.

GROS.   Conceive me, if you can,
A matter-of-fact young man,
An alphabetical, arithmetical,
Every-day young man!

IOLANTHE

ACT I

Good morrow, good mother!
  Good mother, good morrow!
By some means or other,
  Pray banish your sorrow!
    With joy beyond telling
    My bosom is swelling,
    So join in a measure
    Expressive of pleasure,
For I'm to be married today—today—
  Yes, I'm to be married today!

The law is the true embodiment
Of everything that's excellent.
It has no kind of fault or flaw,
And I, my Lords, embody the law.
The constitutional guardian I
Of pretty young Wards in Chancery,
All very agreeable girls—and none
Are over the age of twenty-one.
  A pleasant occupation for
  A rather susceptible Chancellor!

But though the compliment implied
Inflates me with legitimate pride,
It nevertheless can't be denied
That it has its inconvenient side.
For I'm not so old, and not so plain,
And I'm quite prepared to marry again,
But there'd be the deuce to pay in the Lords
If I fell in love with one of my wards!
  Which rather tries my temper, for

I'm *such* a susceptible Chancellor!

And everyone who'd marry a ward
Must come to me for my accord,
And in my court I sit all day,
Giving agreeable girls away,
With one for him—and one for he—
And one for you—and one for ye—
And one for thou—and one for thee—
But never, oh, never a one for me!
    Which is exasperating for
    A highly susceptible Chancellor!

ACT II

SONG—PRIVATE WILLIS

When all night long a chap remains
    On sentry-go, to chase monotony
He exercises of his brains,
    That is, assuming that he's got any.
Though never nurtured in the lap
    Of luxury, yet I admonish you,
I am an intellectual chap,
    And think of things that would astonish you.
        I often think it's comical—Fal, lal, la!
        How nature always does contrive—Fal, lal, la!
            That every boy and every gal
                That's born into the world alive
            Is either a little Liberal
                Or else a little Conservative!
                        Fal, lal, la!

When in that House M.P.'s divide,
    If they've a brain and cerebellum, too,
They've got to leave that brain outside,
    And vote just as their leaders tell 'em to.
But then the prospect of a lot
    Of dull M.P.'s in close proximity,

All thinking for themselves, is what
No man can face with equanimity.
Then let's rejoice with loud Fal la—Fal lal la!
That Nature always does contrive—Fal lal la!
That every boy and every gal
That's born into the world alive
Is either a little Liberal
Or else a little Conservative!
Fal lal la!

SCENE—FAIRIES, *with* LEILA *and* CELIA; PEERS, *with* LORD
MOUNTARARAT *and* LORD TOLLOLLER

LEILA
In vain to us you plead—
Don't go!
Your prayers we do not heed—
Don't go!
It's true we sigh,
But don't suppose
A tearful eye
Forgiveness shows.
Oh, no!
We're very cross indeed—
Don't go!

CELIA
Your disrespectful sneers—
Don't go!
Call forth indignant tears—
Don't go!
You break our laws—
You are our foe:
We cry because
We hate you so!
You know!
You very wicked Peers!
Don't go!

FAIRIES
You break our laws—
You are our foe:

We cry because
We hate you so!
You know!
You very wicked Peers!
Don't go!

MOUNT. *and*   Our disrespectful sneers,
TOLL.   Ha, ha!
Call forth indignant tears,
                                   Ha, ha!
If that's the case, my dears—
FAIRIES   Don't go!
PEERS   We'll go!

SONG—LORD CHANCELLOR

When you're lying awake with a dismal headache, and repose is
    taboo'd by anxiety,
I conceive you may use any language you choose to indulge in,
    without impropriety;
For your brain is on fire—the bedclothes conspire of usual slumber
    to plunder you:
First your counterpane goes, and uncovers your toes, and your sheet
    slips demurely from under you;
Then the blanketing tickles—you feel like mixed pickles—so terribly
    sharp is the pricking,
And you're hot and you're cross, and you tumble and toss till there's
    nothing 'twixt you and the ticking.
Then the bedclothes all creep to the ground in a heap, and you pick
    'em all up in a tangle;
Next your pillow resigns and politely declines to remain at its
    usual angle!
Well, you get some repose in the form of a doze, with hot eye-balls
    and head ever aching.
But your slumbering teems with such horrible dreams that you'd very
    much better be waking;
For you dream you are crossing the Channel, and tossing about in a
    steamer from Harwich—
Which is something between a large bathing machine and a very small
    second-class carriage—

And you're giving a treat (penny ice and cold meat) to a party of
   friends and relations—
They're a ravenous horde—and they all came on board at Sloane
   Square and South Kensington Stations.
And bound on that journey you find your attorney (who started that
   morning from Devon);
He's a bit undersized, and you don't feel surprised when he tells you
   he's only eleven.
Well, you're driving like mad with this singular lad (by the by, the
   ship's now a four-wheeler),
And you're playing round games, and he calls you bad names when
   you tell him that "ties pay the dealer";
But this you can't stand, so you throw up your hand, and you find
   you're as cold as an icicle,
In your shirt and your socks (the black silk with gold clocks),
   crossing Salisbury Plain on a bicycle:
And he and the crew are on bicycles too—which they've somehow or
   other invested in—
And he's telling the tars all the particu*lars* of a company he's
   interested in—
It's a scheme of devices to get at low prices all goods from cough
   mixtures to cables
(Which tickled the sailors), by treating retailers as though they were
   all vege*t*ables—
You get a good spadesman to plant a small tradesman (first take off
   his hoots with a boot-tree),
And his legs will take root, and his fingers will shoot, and they'll
   blossom and bud like a fruit-tree—
From the greengrocer tree you get grapes and green pea, cauliflower,
   pineapple, and cranberries,
While the pastrycook plant cherry brandy will grant, apple puffs and
   three-corners and Banbury's—
The shares are a penny, and ever so many are taken by Rothschild and
   Baring,
And just as a few are allotted to you, you awake with a shudder
   despairing—
You're a regular wreck, with a crick in your neck, and no wonder you
   snore, for your head's on the floor, and you've needles and pins
   from your soles to your shins, and your flesh is a-creep, for your

left leg's asleep, and you've cramp in your toes and a fly on your nose, and some fluff in your lung, and a feverish tongue, and a thirst that's intense, and a general sense that you haven't been sleeping in clover;
But the darkness has passed, and it's daylight at last, and the night has been long—ditto ditto my song—and thank goodness they're both of them over!

PRINCESS IDA

ACT I

SONG—HILARION

Ida was a twelvemonth old,
　　Twenty years ago!
I was twice her age, I'm told,
　　Twenty years ago!
Husband twice as old as wife
Argues ill for married life.
Baleful prophecies were rife,
　　Twenty years ago!

Still, I was a tiny prince
　　Twenty years ago.
She has gained upon me since
　　Twenty years ago.
Though she's twenty-one, it's true,
I am barely twenty-two—
False and foolish prophets you,
　　Twenty years ago!

SONG—ARAC, *with* GURON *and* SCYNTHIUS

ARAC

We are warriors three,
　　Sons of Gama, Rex.
Like most sons are we,
　　Masculine in sex.

ALL THREE   Yes, yes, yes,
                         Masculine in sex.

ARAC   Politics we bar,
                   They are not our bent;
              On the whole we are
                   Not intelligent.

ALL THREE   No, no no,
                         Not intelligent.

ARAC   But with doughty heart,
                   And with trusty blade
              We can play our part—
                   Fighting is our trade.

ALL THREE   Yes, yes, yes,
                         Fighting is our trade.
              Bold and fierce and strong, ha! ha!
                   For a war we burn,
              With its right or wrong, ha! ha!
                   We have no concern.
              Order comes to fight, ha! ha!
                   Order is obeyed,
              We are men of might, ha! ha!
                   Fighting is our trade.
                         Yes, yes, yes,
              Fighting is our trade, ha! ha!

SONG—KING GAMA

If you give me your attention, I will tell you what I am:
I'm a genuine philanthropist—all other kinds are sham.
Each little fault of temper and each social defect
In my erring fellow-creatures I endeavor to correct.
To all their little weaknesses I open people's eyes;
And little plans to snub the self-sufficient I devise;
I love my fellow-creatures—I do all the good I can—
Yet everybody says I'm such a disagreeable man!
    And I can't think why!

. . . . .

I'm sure I'm no ascetic; I'm as pleasant as can be;
You'll always find me ready with a crushing repartee,
I've an irritating chuckle, I've a celebrated sneer,
I've an entertaining snigger, I've a fascinating leer.
Of everybody's prejudice I know a thing or two;
I can tell a woman's age in half a minute—and I do.
But although I try to make myself as pleasant as I can,
Yet everybody says I am a disagreeable man!
    And I can't think why!

ACT II

SONG—LADY PSYCHE

A lady fair, of lineage high,
Was loved by an ape, in the days gone by.
The maid was radiant as the sun,
The ape was a most unsightly one—
    So it would not do—
    His scheme fell through,
For the maid, when his love took formal shape,
    Expressed such terror
    At his monstrous error,
That he stammered an apology and made his 'scape,
The picture of a disconcerted ape.

With a view to rise in the social scale,
He shaved his bristles, and he docked his tail,
He grew mustachios, and he took his tub,
And he paid a guinea to a toilet club—
    But it would not do,
    The scheme fell through—
For the maid was beauty's fairest queen,
    With golden tresses
    Like a real princess's,
While the ape, despite his razor keen,
Was the apiest ape that ever was seen!

He bought white ties, and he bought dress suits,
He crammed his feet into bright tight boots—
And to start in life on a brand-new plan,
He christened himself Darwinian man!
   But it would not do,
    The scheme fell through—
For the maiden fair, whom the monkey craved,
   Was a radiant being,
   With a brain far-seeing—
While a Darwinian man, though well-behaved,
At best is only a monkey shaved!

ACT III

SONG—KING GAMA

Whene'er I poke
Sarcastic joke
   Replete with malice spiteful,
This people mild
Politely smiled,
   And voted me delightful!

Now when a wight
Sits up all night
   Ill-natured jokes devising,
And all his wiles
Are met with smiles
   It's hard, there's no disguising!

O, don't the days seem lank and long
When all goes right and nothing goes wrong,
And isn't your life extremely flat
With nothing whatever to grumble at!

When German bands
From music stands
   Played Wagner imper*fectly*—
I bade them go—

They didn't say no,
   But off they went directly!

The organ boys
They stopped their noise
   With readiness surprising,
And grinning herds
Of hurdy-gurds
   Retired apologizing!

O, don't the days seem lank and long, etc.

I offered gold
In sums untold
   To all who'd contradict me—
I said I'd pay
A pound a day
   To anyone who kicked me—

I bribed with toys
Great vulgar boys
   To utter something spiteful,
But, bless you, no!
They *would* be so
   Confoundedly politeful!

In short, these aggravating lads,
They tickle my tastes, they feed my fads,
They give me this and they give me that,
And I've nothing whatever to grumble at!

THE MIKADO

ACT I

NANK.   A wandering minstrel I—
        A thing of shreds and patches,
        Of ballads, songs, and snatches,
    And dreamy lullaby!
    My catalogue is long,
        Through every passion ranging,
        And to your humors changing
    I tune my supple song!

    Are you in sentimental mood?
        I'll sigh with you,
            Oh, sorrow, sorrow!
    On maiden's coldness do you brood?
        I'll do so, too—
            Oh, sorrow, sorrow!
    I'll charm your willing ears
    With songs of lovers' fears,
    While sympathetic tears
        My cheeks bedew—
            Oh, sorrow, sorrow!

    But if patriotic sentiment is wanted,
        I've patriotic ballads cut and dried;
    For where'er our country's banner may be planted,
        All other local banners are defied!
    Our warriors, in serried ranks assembled,
        Never quail—or they conceal it if they do—
    And I shouldn't be surprised if nations trembled
        Before the mighty troops of Titipu!

    And if you call for a song of the sea,
        We'll heave the capstan round,
    With a yeo heave ho, for the wind is free,
    Her anchor's a-trip and her helm's a-lee,

Hurrah for the homeward bound!

CHO.   Yeo-ho—heave ho—
       Hurrah for the homeward bound!

NANK.   To lay aloft in a howling breeze
       May tickle a landsman's taste,
    But the happiest hour a sailor sees
       Is when he's down
       In an inland town,
    With his Nancy on his knees, yeo ho!
       And his arm around her waist!

CHO.   Then man the capstan—off we go,
       As the fiddler swings us round,
    With a yeo heave ho
    And a rumbelow,
       Hurrah for the homeward bound!

NANK.   A wandering minstrel I, etc.

SONG—KO-KO

As some day it may happen that a victim must be found,
    I've got a little list—I've got a little list
Of society offenders who might well be underground,
    And who never would be missed—who never would be missed!
There's the pestilential nuisances who write for autographs—
All people who have flabby hands and irritating laughs—
All children who are up in dates and floor you with 'em flat—
All persons who in shaking hands, shake hands with you like *that*—
And all third persons who on spoiling *tête-à-têtes* insist—
    They'd none of 'em be missed—they'd none of 'em be missed!

. . . . .

TRIO—YUM-YUM, PEEP-BO, *and* PITTI-SING, *with* CHORUS

THE THREE   Three little maids from school are we,
       Pert as a school-girl well can be,
       Filled to the brim with girlish glee,
          Three little maids from school!

YUM-YUM	Everything is a source of fun.
PEEP-BO	Nobody's safe, for we care for none!
PITTI-SING	Life is a joke that's just begun.
THE THREE	Three little maids from school!
ALL	Three little maids who, all unwary,
	Come from a ladies' seminary,
	Freed from its genius tutelary—
THE THREE	Three little maids from school!

YUM-YUM	One little maid is a bride, Yum-Yum—
PEEP-BO	Two little maids in attendance come—
PITTI-SING	Three little maids is the total sum.
THE THREE	Three little maids from school!
YUM-YUM	From three little maids take one away.
PEEP-BO	Two little maids remain, and they
PITTI-SING	Won't have to wait very long, they say—
THE THREE	Three little maids from school!

ACT II

SONG—YUM-YUM

The sun, whose rays
Are all ablaze
   With ever-living glory,
Does not deny
His majesty—
   He scorns to tell a story!
He don't exclaim,
"I blush for shame,
   So kindly be indulgent."
But, fierce and bold,
In fiery gold,
   He glories all effulgent!

I mean to rule the earth,
   As he the sky—
We really know our worth,

The sun and I!

Observe his flame,
That placid dame,
    The moon's Celestial Highness;
There's not a trace
Upon her face
    Of diffidence or shyness:
She borrows light
That, through the night,
    Mankind may all acclaim her!
And, truth to tell,
She lights up well,
    So I, for one, don't blame her!

Ah, pray make no mistake,
    We are not shy;
We're very wide awake,
    The moon and I!

SONG—MIKADO

A more humane Mikado never
    Did in Japan exist.
        To nobody second
        I'm certainly reckoned
    A true philanthropist.
It is my very humane endeavor
    To make, to some extent,
        Each evil liver
        A running river
Of harmless merriment.

My object all sublime
I shall achieve in time—
To let the punishment fit the crime—
    The punishment fit the crime;
    And make each prisoner pent
    Unwillingly represent
A source of innocent merriment!
    Of innocent merriment!

All prosy dull society sinners,
　Who chatter and bleat and bore,
　　Are sent to hear sermons
　　From mystical Germans
　Who preach from ten till four.
The amateur tenor, whose vocal villainies
　All desire to shirk,
　　Shall, during off-hours,
　　Exhibit his powers
　To Madame Tussaud's waxwork.

. . . . .

The billiard sharp whom anyone catches,
　His doom's extremely hard—
　　He's made to dwell
　　In a dungeon cell
　On a spot that's always barred.
And there he plays extravagant matches
　In fitless finger-stalls
　　On a cloth untrue,
　　With a twisted cue
　And elliptical billiard balls!

My object all sublime, etc.

DUET—NANKI-POO *and* KO-KO

NANK. The flowers that bloom in the spring, tra la,
　　Breathe promise of merry sunshine—
　As we merrily dance and we sing, tra la,
　We welcome the hope that they bring, tra la,
　　Of a summer of roses and wine.
　　　And that's what we mean when we say that a thing
　　　Is welcome as flowers that bloom in the spring.
　　　　Tra la la la la la, etc.

KO. 　The flowers that bloom in the spring, tra la,
　　Have nothing to do with the case.
　I've got to take under my wing, tra la,
　A most unattractive old thing, tra la,

With a caricature of a face.
    And that's what I mean when I say or I sing,
      "Oh, bother the flowers that bloom in the spring."
        Tra la la la la la, etc.

SONG——KO-KO

On a tree by a river a little tom-tit
    Sang, "Willow, titwillow, titwillow!"
And I said to him, "Dicky-bird, why do you sit
    Singing, 'Willow, titwillow, titwillow'?"
"Is it weakness of intellect, birdie?" I cried,
"Or a rather tough worm in your little inside?"
With a shake of his poor little head, he replied,
    "Oh, willow, titwillow, titwillow!"

He slapped at his chest, as he sat on that bough,
    Singing, "Willow, titwillow, titwillow!"
And a cold perspiration bespangled his brow,
    Oh, willow, titwillow, titwillow!
He sobbed and he sighed, and a gurgle he gave,
Then he plunged himself into the billowy wave,
And an echo arose from the suicide's grave—
    "Oh, willow, titwillow, titwillow!"

Now I feel just as sure as I'm sure that my name
    Isn't Willow, titwillow, titwillow,
That 'twas blighted affection that made him exclaim,
    "Oh, willow, titwillow, titwillow!"
And if you remain callous and obdurate, I
Shall perish as he did, and you will know why,
Though I probably shall not exclaim as I die,
    "Oh, willow, titwillow, titwillow!"

DUET——KATISHA *and* KO-KO

KAT.   There is beauty in the bellow of the blast,
      There is grandeur in the growling of the gale,
        There is eloquent outpouring
        When the lion is a-roaring,
      And the tiger is a-lashing of his tail!

KO.   Yes, I like to see a tiger
        From the Congo or the Niger,
    And especially when lashing of his tail!

KAT.   Volcanoes have a splendor that is grim,
       And earthquakes only terrify the dolts,
         But to him who's scientific
         There's nothing that's terrific
      In the falling of a flight of thunderbolts!

KO.   Yes, in spite of all my meekness,
        If I have a little weakness,
     It's a passion for a flight of thunderbolts!

BOTH   If that is so,
      Sing derry down derry!
      It's evident, very,
        Our tastes are one.
    Away we'll go
      And merrily marry,
      Nor tardily tarry
        Till day is done!

KO.   There is beauty in extreme old age—
      Do you fancy you are elderly enough?
        Information I'm requesting
        On a subject interesting:
      Is a maiden all the better when she's tough?

KAT.   Throughout this wide dominion
        It's the general opinion
      That she'll last a good deal longer when she's tough.

KO.   Are you old enough to marry, do you think?
      Won't you wait till you are eighty in the shade?
        There's a fascination frantic
        In a ruin that's romantic;
      Do you think you are sufficiently decayed?

KAT.   To the matter that you mention
        I have given some attention,
      And I think I am sufficiently decayed.

BOTH   If that is so, etc.

RUDDIGORE

ACT I

If somebody there chanced to be
   Who loved me in a manner true,
My heart would point him out to me,
   And I would point him out to you.
(*Referring*   But here it says of those who point—
to book)   Their manners must be out of joint—
      You *may* not point—
      You *must* not point—
    It's manners out of joint to point!

Had I the love of such as he,
   Some quiet spot he'd take me to,
Then he could whisper it to me,
   And I could whisper it to you.
(*Referring*   But whispering, I've somewhere met,
to book)   Is contrary to etiquette:
      Where can it be?   (*Searching book*)
      Now let me see—   (*Finding reference*)
       Yes, yes!
    It's contrary to etiquette!

If any well-bred youth I knew,
   Polite and gentle, neat and trim,
Then I would hint as much to you,
   And you could hint as much to him.
(*Referring*   But here it says, in plainest print,
to book)   "It's most unladylike to hint"—
      You *may* not hint,
      You *must* not hint—
    It says you mustn't hint, in print!

And if I loved him through and through—
   (True love and not a passing whim),
Then I could speak of it to you,
   And you could speak of it to him.

But here I find it doesn't do
To speak until you're spoken to.
    Where can it be?   (*Searching book*)
    Now let me see—   (*Finding reference*)
      Yes, yes!
"Don't speak until you're spoken to!"

DUET—ROBIN *and* ROSE

ROB.   I know a youth who loves a little maid—
       (Hey, but his face is a sight to see!)
    Silent is he, for he's modest and afraid—
       (Hey, but he's timid as a youth can be!)

ROSE   I know a maid who loves a gallant youth,
       (Hey, but she sickens as the days go by!)
    She cannot tell him all the sad, sad truth—
       (Hey, but I think that little maid will die!)

ROB.   Poor little man!
ROSE   Poor little maid!
ROB.   Poor little man!
ROSE   Poor little maid!
BOTH   Now tell me pray, and tell me true,

What in the world should the $\left\{ \begin{array}{l} \text{young man} \\ \text{maiden} \end{array} \right\}$ do?

ROB.   He cannot eat and he cannot sleep—
       (Hey, but his face is a sight for to see!)
    Daily he goes for to wail—for to weep.
       (Hey, but he's wretched as a youth can be!)

ROSE   She's very thin and she's very pale—
       (Hey, but she sickens as the days go by!)
    Daily she goes for to weep—for to wail—
       (Hey, but I think that little maid will die!)

ROB.   Poor little maid!
ROSE   Poor little man!
ROB.   Poor little maid!
ROSE   Poor little man!
BOTH   Now tell me pray, and tell me true,

What in the world should the $\left\{ \begin{array}{l} \text{young man} \\ \text{maiden} \end{array} \right\}$ do?

ROSE   If I were the youth I should offer her my name—
        (Hey, but her face is a sight for to see!)

ROB.   If I were the maid I should fan his honest flame—
        (Hey, but he's bashful as a youth can be!)

ROSE   If I were the youth I should speak to her today—
        (Hey, but she sickens as the days go by!)

ROB.   If I were the maid I should meet the lad half-way—
        (For I really do believe that timid youth will die!)

ROSE   Poor little man!
ROB.   Poor little maid!
ROSE   Poor little man!
ROB.   Poor little maid!

BOTH   I thank you, $\left\{ \begin{array}{l} \text{miss,} \\ \text{sir,} \end{array} \right\}$ for your counsel true;

       I'll tell that $\left\{ \begin{array}{l} \text{youth} \\ \text{maid} \end{array} \right\}$ what $\left\{ \begin{array}{l} \text{he} \\ \text{she} \end{array} \right\}$ ought to do!

SCENE—MARGARET

Cheerily carols the lark
Over the cot.
Merrily whistles the clerk
Scratching a blot.
But the lark
And the clerk,
I remark,
Comfort me not!

Over the ripening peach
Buzzes the bee.
Splash on the billowy beach
Tumbles the sea.
But the peach
And the beach
They are each
Nothing to me!

And why?
Who am I?
Daft Madge! Crazy Meg!

Mad Margaret! Poor Peg!
He! he! he! he! he!

Mad, I?
Yes, very?
But why?
Mystery!
Don't call!
Whisht! whisht!
No crime—
'Tis only
That I'm
Love-lonely!
That's all!

To a garden full of posies
  Cometh one to gather flowers,
  And he wanders through its bowers
Toying with the wanton roses,
  Who, uprising from their beds,
  Hold on high their shameless heads
With their pretty lips a-pouting,
Never doubting—never doubting
  That for Cytherean posies
  He would gather aught but roses!

In a nest of weeds and nettles
  Lay a violet, half-hidden,
  Hoping that his glance unbidden
Yet might fall upon her petals.
  Though she lived alone, apart,
  Hope lay nestling at her heart,
But, alas, the cruel waking
Set her little heart a-breaking,
  For he gathered for his posies
  Only roses—only roses!

ACT II

SONG—SIR RODERIC *and* CHORUS

When the night wind howls in the chimney cowls, and the bat
    in the moonlight flies,
And inky clouds, like funeral shrouds, sail over the midnight
    skies—
When the footpads quail at the night-bird's wail, and black
    dogs bay at the moon,
Then is the specter's holiday—then is the ghosts' high-noon!

CHO.
        Ha! ha!
    Then is the ghosts' high-noon!

As the sob of the breeze sweeps over the trees, and the mists
    lie low on the fen,
From grey tombstones are gathered the bones that once were
    women and men,
And away they go, with a mop and mow, to the revel that ends
    too soon,
For cockcrow limits our holiday—the dead of the night's
    high-noon!

CHO.
        Ha! ha!
    The dead of the night's high-noon!

And then each ghost with his ladye-toast to their churchyard
    bed takes flight,
With a kiss, perhaps, on her lantern chaps, and a grisly
    grim "good-night";
Till the welcome knell of the midnight bell rings forth its
    jolliest tune,
And ushers in our next high holiday—the dead of the night's
    high-noon!

CHO.
        Ha! ha!
    The dead of the night's high-noon!

TRIO—ROBIN, DESPARD, *and* MARGARET

ROB.   My eyes are fully open to my awful situation—

I shall go at once to Roderic and make him an oration.
I shall tell him I've recovered my forgotten moral senses,
And I don't care twopence-halfpenny for any consequences.
Now I do not want to perish by the sword or by the dagger,
But a martyr may indulge a little pardonable swagger,
And a word or two of compliment my vanity would flatter,
But I've got to die tomorrow, so it really doesn't matter!

DES.   So it really doesn't matter—
MAR.   So it really doesn't matter—
ALL   So it really doesn't matter, matter, matter, matter, matter!

MAR.   If I were not a little mad and generally silly
I should give you my advice upon the subject, willy-nilly;
I should show you in a moment how to grapple with the
        question,
And you'd really be astonished at the force of my suggestion.
On the subject I shall write you a most valuable letter,
Full of excellent suggestions when I feel a little better,
But at present I'm afraid I am as mad as any hatter,
So I'll keep 'em to myself, for my opinion doesn't matter!

DES.   Her opinion doesn't matter—
ROB.   Her opinion doesn't matter—
ALL   Her ⎫
        My ⎬ opinion doesn't matter, matter, matter, matter, matter!

DES.   If I had been so lucky as to have a steady brother
Who could talk to me as we are talking now to one another—
Who could give me good advice when he discovered I was
        erring
(Which is just the very favor which on you I am conferring),
My story would have made a rather interesting idyll,
And I might have lived and died a very decent indiwiddle.
This particularly rapid, unintelligible patter
Isn't generally heard, and if it is it doesn't matter!

ROB.   If it is it doesn't matter—
MAR.   If it ain't it doesn't matter—
ALL   If it ⎧ ain't ⎫ it doesn't matter, matter, matter, matter, matter!
              ⎩ is   ⎭

SONG—HANNAH

There grew a little flower
　'Neath a great oak tree:
When the tempest 'gan to lower
　Little heeded she:
No need had she to cower,
For she dreaded not its power—
She was happy in the bower
　Of her great oak tree!
　　Sing hey,
　　Lackaday!
　Let the tears fall free
For the pretty little flower
　And the great oak tree!

When she found that he was fickle,
　Was that great oak tree,
She was in a pretty pickle,
　As she well might be—
But his gallantries were mickle,
For Death followed with his sickle,
And her tears began to trickle
　For her great oak tree!
　　Sing hey, etc.

Said she, "He loved me never,
　Did that great oak tree,
But I'm neither rich nor clever,
　And so why should he?
But though fate our fortunes sever,
To be constant I'll endeavor,
Aye, forever and forever,
　To my great oak tree!"
　　Sing hey, etc.

THE YEOMEN OF THE GUARD

ACT I

Is life a boon?
  If so, it must befall,
  That Death, whene'er he call,
Must call too soon.
  Though fourscore years he give,
  Yet one would pray to live
Another moon!
  What kind of plaint have I,
  Who perish in July?
  I might have had to die,
Perchance, in June!

Is life a thorn?
  Then count it not a whit!
  Man is well done with it;
Soon as he's born
  He should all means essay
  To put the plague away;
And I, war-worn,
  Poor captured fugitive,
  My life most gladly give—
  I might have had to live
Another morn!

DUET—JACK POINT *and* ELSIE

POINT   I have a song to sing, O!

ELSIE   Sing me your song, O!

POINT   It is sung to the moon
            By a lovelorn loon,
      Who fled from the mocking throng, O!
      It's a song of a merryman, moping mum,

Whose soul was sad, and whose glance was glum,
Who sipped no sup, and who craved no crumb,
  As he sighed for the love of a ladye.

BOTH   Heighdy! heighdy!
           Misery me, lackadaydee!
He sipped no sup, and he craved no crumb,
  As he sighed for the love of a ladye.

ELSIE   I have a song to sing, O!

POINT   What is your song, O?

ELSIE   It is sung with the ring
         Of the songs maids sing
    Who love with a love life-long, O!
It's the song of a merrymaid, peerly proud,
Who loved a lord and who laughed aloud
At the moan of the merryman, moping mum,
Whose soul was sad, and whose glance was glum,
Who sipped no sup, and who craved no crumb,
  As he sighed for the love of a ladye.

BOTH   Heighdy! heighdy!
           Misery me, lackadaydee!
He sipped no sup, etc.

POINT   I have a song to sing, O!

ELSIE   Sing me your song, O!

POINT   It is sung to the knell
         Of a churchyard bell,
    And a doleful dirge, ding dong, O!
It's a song of a popinjay, bravely born,
Who turned up his noble nose with scorn
At the humble merrymaid, peerly proud,
Who loved a lord, and who laughed aloud
At the moan of a merryman, moping mum,
Whose soul was sad, and whose glance was glum,
Who sipped no sup, and who craved no crumb,
  As he sighed for the love of a ladye.

BOTH   Heighdy! heighdy!
           Misery me, lackadaydee!

He sipped no sup, etc.

ELSIE   I have a song to sing, O!

POINT   Sing me your song, O!

ELSIE
     It is sung with a sigh
     And a tear in the eye,
  For it tells of a righted wrong, O!
It's a song of the merrymaid, once so gay,
Who turned on her heel and tripped away
From the peacock popinjay, bravely born,
Who turned up his noble nose with scorn
At the humble heart that he did not prize:
So she begged on her knees, with downcast eyes,
For the love of the merryman, moping mum,
Whose soul was sad, and whose glance was glum,
Who sipped no sup, and who craved no crumb,
  As he sighed for the love of a ladye.

BOTH
     Heighdy! heighdy!
     Misery me, lackadaydee!
His pains were o'er, and he sighed no more,
For he lived in the love of a ladye.

SONG—PHOEBE

Were I thy bride,
Then all the world beside
Were not too wide
To hold my wealth of love—
Were I thy bride!

Upon thy breast
My loving head would rest,
As on her nest
The tender turtle dove—
Were I thy bride!

This heart of mine
Would be one heart with thine,
And in that shrine

Our happiness would dwell—
Were I thy bride!

And all day long
Our lives should be a song:
  No grief, no wrong
    Should make my heart rebel—
Were I thy bride!

The silvery flute,
The melancholy lute,
  Were night-owl's hoot
    To my low-whispered coo—
Were I thy bride!

The skylark's trill
Were but discordance shrill
  To the soft thrill
    Of wooing as I'd woo—
Were I thy bride!

The rose's sigh
Were as a carrion's cry
  To lullaby
    Such as I'd sing to thee,
Were I thy bride!

A feather's press
Were leaden heaviness
  To my caress.
    But then, of course, you see,
I'm not thy bride!

ACT II

SONG—JACK POINT

Oh! a private buffoon is a lighthearted loon,
  If you listen to popular rumor;
From the morn to the night he's so joyous and bright,
  And he bubbles with wit and good-humor!

He's so quaint and so terse, both in prose and in verse;
  Yet though people forgive his transgression,
There are one or two rules that all family fools
  Must observe, if they love their profession.
      There are one or two rules,
        Half a dozen, may be,
      That all family fools,
        Of whatever degree,
  Must observe, if they love their profession.

If you wish to succeed as a jester, you'll need
  To consider each person's auricular:
What is all right for B would quite scandalize C
  (For C is so very particular);
And D may be dull, and E's very thick skull
  Is as empty of brains as a ladle;
While F is F sharp, and will cry with a carp
  That he's known your best joke from his cradle!
      When your humor they flout,
        You can't let yourself go;
      And it *does* put you out
        When a person says, "Oh,
  I have known that old joke from my cradle!"

If your master is surly, from getting up early
  (And tempers are short in the morning),
An inopportune joke is enough to provoke
  Him to give you, at once, a month's warning.
Then if you refrain, he is at you again,
  For he likes to get value for money;
He'll ask then and there, with an insolent stare,
  If you know that you're paid to be funny.
      It adds to the tasks
        Of a merryman's place,
      When your principal asks,
        With a scowl on his face,
  If you know that you're paid to be funny.

· · · · ·

Though your head it may rack with a bilious attack,

And your senses with toothache you're losing,
Don't be mopy and flat—they don't fine you for that,
   If you're properly quaint and amusing!
Though your wife ran away with a soldier that day,
   And took with her your trifle of money;
Bless your heart, they don't mind—they're exceedingly kind—
   They don't blame you—as long as you're funny!
    It's a comfort to feel,
      If your partner should flit,
   Though *you* suffer a deal,
     They don't mind it a bit—
They don't blame you—so long as you're funny!

THE GONDOLIERS

ACT I

DUET—MARCO *and* GIUSEPPE

We're called *gondolieri*,
But that's a vagary,
It's quite honorary
   The trade that we ply.
For gallantry noted
Since we were short-coated,
To beauty devoted,
  Giuseppe ⎱
  Are Marco ⎰ and I;

When morning is breaking,
Our couches forsaking,
To greet their awaking
   With carols we come,
At summer day's nooning,
When weary lagooning,
Our mandolins tuning,
   We lazily thrum.

When vespers are ringing,
To hope ever clinging,
With songs of our singing
A vigil we keep,
When daylight is fading,
Enwrapt in night's shading,
With soft serenading
We sing them to sleep.

SCENE—DUKE, DUCHESS, CASILDA, *and* LUIZ

DUKE From the sunny Spanish shore,
The Duke of Plaza Tor'—

DUCH. And His Grace's Duchess true—

CAS. And His Grace's daughter, too—

LUIZ And His Grace's private drum
To Venetia's shores have come:

ALL If ever, ever, ever
They get back to Spain,
They will never, never, never
Cross the sea again—

DUKE Neither that grandee from the Spanish shore,
The noble Duke of Plaza Tor'—

DUCH. Nor His Grace's Duchess, staunch and true—

CAS. You may add His Grace's daughter, too—

LUIZ Nor His Grace's own particular drum
To Venetia's shores will come:

ALL If ever, ever, ever
They get back to Spain,
They will never, never, never
Cross the sea again!

SONG—DON ALHAMBRA

I stole the prince and brought him here,

And left him gaily prattling
With a highly respectable gondolier,
Who promised the royal babe to rear,
And teach him the trade of a timoneer
   With his own beloved bratling.

Both of the babes were strong and stout,
   And, considering all things, clever.
Of that there is no manner of doubt—
No probable, possible shadow of doubt—
   No possible doubt whatever.

But owing, I'm much disposed to fear,
   To his terrible taste for tippling,
That highly respectable gondolier
Could never declare with a mind sincere
Which of the two was his offspring dear,
   And which was the royal stripling!

Which was which he could never make out,
   Despite his best endeavor.
Of *that* there is no manner of doubt—
No probable, possible shadow of doubt—
   No possible doubt whatever.

Time sped, and when at the end of a year
   I sought the infant cherished,
That highly respectable gondolier
Was lying a corpse on his humble bier—
I dropped a Grand Inquisitor's tear—
   That gondolier had perished.

A taste for drink combined with gout,
   Had doubled him up forever.
Of *that* there is no manner of doubt—
No probable, possible shadow of doubt—
   No possible doubt whatever.

The children followed his old career—
   (This statement can't be parried)
Of a highly respectable gondolier;

Well, one of the two (who will soon be here)—
But *which* of the two is not quite clear—
  Is the royal prince you married!

Search in and out and round about,
  And you'll discover never
A tale so free from every doubt—
All probable, possible shadow of doubt—
  All possible doubt whatever!

SONG—TESSA

When a merry maiden marries,
Sorrow goes and pleasure tarries;
  Every sound becomes a song,
  All is right, and nothing's wrong!
From today and ever after
Let our tears be tears of laughter.
  Every sigh that finds a vent
  Be a sigh of sweet content!
When you marry, merry maiden,
Then the air with love is laden;
  Every flower is a rose,
    Every goose becomes a swan,
  Every kind of trouble goes
    Where the last year's snows have gone!

When a merry maiden marries,
Sorrow goes and pleasure tarries;
  Every sound becomes a song,
  All is right, and nothing's wrong.
Gnawing care and aching sorrow,
Get ye gone until tomorrow;
  Jealousies in grim array,
  Ye are things of yesterday!
When you marry, merry maiden,
Then the air with joy is laden;
  All the corners of the earth
    Ring with music sweetly played,
  Worry is melodious mirth,
    Grief is joy in masquerade.

ACT II

SONG——MARCO

Take a pair of sparkling eyes
  Hidden, ever and anon,
    In a merciful eclipse—
Do not heed their mild surprise—
  Having passed the Rubicon,
    Take a pair of rosy lips;
Take a figure trimly planned—
  Such as admiration whets
    (Be particular in this);
Take a tender little hand
  Fringed with dainty fingerettes,
    Press it—in parenthesis;—
Ah! Take all these, you lucky man—
Take and keep them, if you can!

Take a pretty little cot—
  Quite a miniature affair—
    Hung about with trellised vine,
Furnish it upon the spot
  With the treasures rich and rare
    I've endeavored to define.
Live to love and love to live—
  You will ripen at your ease,
    Growing on the sunny side—
Fate has nothing more to give.
  You're a dainty man to please
    If you are not satisfied.
Ah! Take my counsel, happy man;
Act upon it, if you can!

Index

Alexis, 22-31
Alhambra del Bolero, Don,
    166-175
  song, 236-238
Aline, 22-31
Angela, 66-79
  duet, 201-202
Angelina, 14-19
Arac, 99
  song, 211-212

Bab Ballads, 2, 33, 81
Blanche, Lady, 101-108
Boatswain, 34, 38, 43
  scene, 193
Bunthorne, Reginald, 66-79
  duet, 204-205
  song, 200-201
Buttercup, *see* Little Buttercup

Carruthers, Dame, 146-160

Casilda, 164-175
  scene, 236
Celia, 82, 89
  scene, 208
Chloe, 101, 107
Cholmondeley, Sir Richard,
    148-160
Clay, Fred, 1
Constance, 22-31
  song, 183-184
Corcoran, Captain, 35-45
  duet, 189-191
  songs, 186-187, 189
  trio, 191-192
Counsel for the Plaintiff, 16-19
  song, 179
Cyril, 98-109

Daly, Dr., 22-31
  song, 180-181
Despard, *see* Murgatroyd, Sir
    Despard

Dick Deadeye, 34, 38, 41-43
D'Oyly Carte, Richard, 6-10, 13,
    21, 81
Dunstable, Duke of, 68, 75

Edith, 53
    scene, 198-199
Edwin, 14-19
    songs, 177-178, 180
Ella, 66-79
Elsie, *see* Maynard, Elsie

Fairfax, Colonel, 146-161
    song, 230
Fifth Avenue Theatre (New
    York), 49
Fleta, 82
Florian, 98-109
Frederic, 50-53, 56-60
    song, 196
Fun (periodical), 2, 13

Gama, King, 98-109
    songs, 212-213, 214-215
Gianetta, 164-175
Gilbert, William S., 1-11, 13, 21,
    33, 49, 65, 81, 97, 111, 129,
    145, 163
Giuseppe, 164-175
    duet, 235-236
Gondoliers, The, 9, 163-175
    songs, 235-239
Goodheart, Old Adam, 133, 136,
    139, 141
Grand Duke, The, 10-11
Grosvenor, Archibald, 70-78
    duets, 202, 204-205
    song, 203
Guron, 99
    song, 211-212

Hannah, Dame, 131-143
    song, 229

Hebe, Cousin, 37, 40, 44
Hilarion, Prince, 98-109
    song, 211
Hildebrand, King, 98-100,
    105-108
H.M.S. Pinafore, 6-7, 33-46
    songs, 185-193

Ida, Princess, 98-109
Iolanthe, 7, 81-95
    songs, 206-211
Iolanthe, 82-94
Isabel, 53
Ivanhoe, 10

Jane, Lady, 66-79
    song, 203
Josephine, 36-45
    duet, 188-189
    scene, 193
    trio, 191-192
Judge, 14-19
    song, 178-179

Kate, 53
Katisha, 115, 118, 123, 125-128
    duet, 221-222
Ko-Ko, 112-128
    duets, 220-222
    songs, 217, 221

Leila, 82-94
    scene, 208
Little Buttercup, 34-46
    songs, 185, 189-191, 193-194
Lord Chancellor, 85-95
    songs, 206-207, 209-211
Luiz, 164-175
    scene, 236

Mabel, 53-54, 56-59
    scene, 198-199
    song, 197

Marco, 164-175
  duet, 235-236
  song, 239
Major-General, *see* Stanley,
  General
Margaret, Mad, 135-143
  scene, 225-226
  trio, 227-228
Maynard, Elsie, 149-161
  duet, 230-232
Melissa, 100-109
Meryll, Leonard, 147-161
Meryll, Phoebe, 146-160
  song, 232-233
Meryll, Sergeant, 146-160
Mikado, 112-128
  song, 219-220
Mikado, The, 8-9, 111-128, 129,
  songs, 216-222
Mountararat, Lord, 86-95
  scene, 208-209
Murgatroyd, Sir Despard,
  135-143
  trio, 227-228
Murgatroyd, Richard, 133-143
Murgatroyd, Sir Roderic,
  131-143
  song, 227

Nanki-Poo, 112-128
  duet, 220-221
  song, 216-217

Oakapple, Robin, 132-143
  duet, 224-225
  trio, 227-228
Opéra Comique Theatre
  (London), 6, 7, 21, 33, 49, 65

Palace Music Hall (London), 10
Partlet, Mrs., 22-31

Patience, 66-78
  duets, 201-202
Patience, 6, 65-79
Peep-Bo, 114, 118
  trio, 217-218
Périchole, La, 6
Phoebe, *see* Meryll, Phoebe
Phyllis, 83-95
Pinafore, see *H.M.S. Pinafore*
Pirate King, 50-62
  song, 195-196
Pirates of Penzance, The, 7, 49-62
  songs, 194-200
Pish-Tush, 112
Pitti-Sing, 114-128
  trio, 217-218
Plaza-Toro, Duchess of, 164-174
  scene, 236
Plaza-Toro, Duke of, 164-174
  scene, 236
Point, Jack, 149-161
  duet, 230-232
  song, 233-235
Pointdextre, Sir Marmaduke,
  22-31
Pooh-Bah, 113-128
Porter, Sir Joseph, 36-46
  song, 187-188
  trio, 191-192
Princess, The (play), 97
Princess Ida, 7, 97-109, 111
  songs, 211-215
Psyche, Lady, 100-109
  song, 213-214

Rackstraw, Ralph, 34-35, 38-40,
  43-45
  duet, 188-189
  scene, 193
  song, 186
Robin, *see* Oakapple, Robin

Roderic, *see* Murgatroyd, Sir
    Roderic
Rose Maybud, 131-143
    duet, 224-225
    song, 223-224
Royal English Opera House
    (London), 10
Royalty Theatre (London), 6, 13
Ruddigore, 9, 129-143
    songs, 223-229
Ruth, 50-53, 56-58, 62
    song, 194-195

Sacharissa, 100, 107
Sailors' Chorus, 185
Sangazure, Lady, 22-31
    duet, 184
Saphir, 66-79
Savoy Theatre (London), 7, 8,
    10, 81, 97, 111, 129, 145, 163
Scott, Sir Walter, 10
Scynthius, 99
    song 211-212
Sergeant, 57
    scene, 198
    song, 200
Shadbolt, Wilfred, 146, 147,
    150-154
Sorcerer, The, 6, 11, 21-31
    songs, 180-184
Samuel, 51, 54

Stanley, General, 54-58, 62
    song, 197-198
Strephon, 83-89
    song, 206
Sullivan, Arthur, 1-11, 13, 21, 33,
    49, 97, 111, 129, 145, 163
Sullivan, Frederic, 6

Tessa, 164-175
    song, 238
Thespis, 5, 6, 13
Tolloller, Lord, 86-95
    scene, 208-209
Trial by Jury, 6, 13-19
    songs, 177-180

Victoria, Queen, 7

Wells, John Wellington, 24-31
    duet, 184
    song, 181-183
Willis, Private, 90-95
    song, 207-208

Yeoman of the Guard, The, 9,
    145-161
    songs, 230-235
Yum-Yum, 112-128
    song, 218-219
    trio, 217-218

Zorah, 131-143

Index of First Lines

A lady fair, of lineage high, 213
A magnet hung in a hardware shop, 203
A maiden fair to see, 186
A many years ago, 193
A more humane Mikado never, 219
A wandering minstrel I, 216
As some day it may happen that a victim must be found, 217

Cheerily carols the lark, 225

Dear friends, take pity on my lot, 183

Fair moon, to thee I sing, 189
For I'm called Little Buttercup— dear little Buttercup, 185
From the sunny Spanish shore, 236

Good morrow, good mother, 206

Hate me! I drop my H's—have through life, 184

I am the captain of the *Pinafore*, 186
I am the very model of a modern Major-General, 197
I have a song to sing, O, 230
I, humble, poor, and lowly born, 193
I know a youth who loves a little maid, 224
I stole the prince and brought him here, 236
Ida was a twelvemonth old, 211
If somebody there chanced to be, 223
If you give me your attention, I will tell you what I am, 212

245

If you're anxious for to shine in the high aesthetic line as a man of culture rare, 200

In vain to us you plead, 208

Is life a boon, 230

Long years ago—fourteen, maybe, 201

My eyes are fully open to my awful situation, 227

My name is John Wellington Wells, 181

Never mind the why and wherefore, 191

Oh! a private buffoon is a light-hearted loon, 233

Oh, better far to live and die, 195

Oh, gentlemen, listen, I pray, 180

Oh, is there not one maiden breast, 196

On a tree by a river a little tom-tit, 221

Poor wandering one, 197

Prithee, pretty maiden—prithee, tell me true, 202

Refrain, audacious tar, 188

Silvered is the raven hair, 203

Take a pair of sparkling eyes, 239

The flowers that bloom in the spring, tra la, 220

The law is the true embodiment, 206

The sun, whose rays, 218

There grew a little flower, 229

There is beauty in the bellow of the blast, 221

Things are seldom what they seem, 189

Three little maids from school are we, 217

Time was when Love and I were well acquainted, 180

To a garden full of posies, 226

We are warriors three, 211

We sail the ocean blue, 185

We're called *gondolieri*, 235

Were I thy bride, 232

When a felon's not engaged in his employment, 200

When a merry maiden marries, 238

When all night long a chap remains, 207

When first my old, old love I knew, 177

When Frederic was a little lad he proved so brave and daring, 194

When I go out of door, 204

When I, good friends, was called to the bar, 178

When I was a lad I served a term, 187

When the foeman bares his steel, 198

When the night wind howls in the chimney cowls, and the bat in the moonlight flies, 227

When you're lying awake with a dismal headache, and repose is taboo'd by anxiety, 209

When'er I poke, 214

With a sense of deep emotion, 179

ABOUT THE AUTHOR

Clyde Robert Bulla was born near King City, Missouri. His formal education began in a one-room schoolhouse, where he wrote his first stories and composed his first songs.

Music, and opera in particular, has always been an important part of Mr. Bulla's life. His books about opera include *Stories of Favorite Operas*, *More Stories of Favorite Operas*, and *The Ring and the Fire*, which recounts the legend of Wagner's famous Nibelung cycle.

Mr. Bulla lives in Los Angeles, California.

ABOUT THE ILLUSTRATORS

In the cellar of the McCrea home, there is a small sixty-year-old hand press. Mr. and Mrs. McCrea use it to prepare Christmas booklets, block prints, and broadsides, many of which bear the imprint of The Little Press. They also use the press to print the type for children's books that they have written, designed, and illustrated.

Ruth McCrea was born in Jersey City, New Jersey. Her husband is a native of Peoria, Illinois. They both attended the Ringling School of Art in Sarasota, Florida, and took night classes at New York University and at the Brooklyn Museum. Mr. and Mrs. McCrea each grew up with an interest in writing and drawing. Since they met in art school, they have been working together on jacket design, writing, and illustrating. Mr. McCrea has also done book design and for several years taught typography at Cooper Union in New York City. Mrs. McCrea has illustrated many books on her own.

The McCreas, who have a son and two daughters, live in Bayport, New York.